Magnificence and Awe

RENAISSANCE *and* BAROQUE ART
in the VIOLA E. BRAY GALLERY
at the FLINT INSTITUTE OF ARTS

MAGNIFICENCE

and AWE

RENAISSANCE *and* BAROQUE ART

in the VIOLA E. BRAY GALLERY

at the FLINT INSTITUTE OF ARTS

Essays by Arnauld Brejon de Lavergnée, Charissa Bremer-David, Tracee J. Glab, *and* John B. Henry, III

Magnificence and Awe: Renaissance and Baroque Art in the Viola E. Bray Gallery at the Flint Institute of Arts was published in celebration of the fiftieth anniversary opening of the Viola E. Bray Gallery.

Publication made possible through the generosity of
The Whiting Foundation
The Samuel H. Kress Foundation
The Viola E. Bray Charitable Trust
An anonymous grant in honor of Piper Realty Company,
celebrating 90 years and 4 generations of leadership in
fine real estate in Michigan

Printed in the United States of America
Library of Congress Control Number: 2011932282
ISBN 978-0-578-08755-9

Published by the Flint Institute of Arts
1120 E. Kearsley Street
Flint, Michigan 48503-1991
www.flintarts.org

Director: John B. Henry, III
Coordinator of Collections and Exhibitions: Michael Martin
Associate Curator: Tracee J. Glab
Photography (unless otherwise noted) by Robert Hensleigh
and Tim Thayer
Designed by Savitski Design, Ann Arbor, Michigan
Edited by Stephen Robert Frankel
Index by Monica Rumsey
Printed by Spartan Printing, Lansing, Michigan

Frontispiece: From left to right: Simon Vouet, French (1590–1649), designer; woven at the Faubourg Saint-Germain tapestry workshop (1633–67/68), "Carlo and Ubaldo Spy on the Lovers," from *The Story of Rinaldo and Armida* tapestry cycle, 1633–37 (detail of cat. 5); Spanish, *Candlestick*, 17th century (cat. 21)

Page vi–vii: Viola E. Bray Gallery at the Flint Institute of Arts.

Page 51: Giovanni Buora, Italian (ca. 1450–1513), *Angel Holding Candlestick* (one of a pair), late 15th, early 16th century (detail of cat. 15a)

Contents

Foreword and Acknowledgments

This publication is in celebration of the fiftieth anniversary of the Viola E. Bray Gallery, which opened on November 7, 1961,[1] in a new wing of the DeWaters Art Center, home to the Flint Institute of Arts. The gallery was specifically designed to hold the Renaissance and Baroque objects collected by a single individual—nearly sixty works, including tapestries, a painting, sculpture, furniture, ceramics, and bronzes. These works, along with their unique architectural space, were given by Viola E. Bray, a Flint native, avid art collector, and philanthropist.

Until now, the only available document of the collection was the 1963 publication dedicated to the Viola E. Bray Gallery, with a foreword by then-director G. Stuart Hodge.[2] That 37-page booklet included only brief explanatory texts and reproduced the works in black-and-white, which could not begin to do justice to how the works look when they are encountered in "living" color in the museum. However, when viewing the works in the Viola E. Bray Gallery in the low-light conditions required to protect the tapestries, it is impossible to see many of the details. With this book, we offer a closer look than is possible in person, provide useful and fascinating information, focus on aspects of the works that may not be noticed at first glance, and bring attention to details that are essential to making connections among the objects in the collection (see figs. 1, 2). This current publication presents these objects—most for the first time—in color, using the latest digital photography, along with the most up-to-date research. It is our hope that it will generate public and scholarly interest in these works, as well as highlight the importance of this gift in the context of mid-twentieth-century American collecting practices.

This book would not have been possible without the generous support of individuals and institutions locally, across the country, and abroad, and I have many people to thank for contributing their time, expertise, and financial support. I wish to express my sincere appreciation to those individuals and foundations that provided the funds needed to complete the project. I am most grateful to Max Marmor and the Samuel H. Kress Foundation for their generous lead grant. From the start, it has been our intention to bring new insight into the materials and physical attributes of these works in order to facilitate research by scholars who cannot come to Flint in person to see the collection. As part of this project, the foundation awarded the FIA a History of Art grant, which included funding for digital photography. The resulting 21-megapixel photographs not only document the collection more accurately, but also, for the first time, reveal many aspects of the works in astounding detail.

Fig. 1. Detail of cat. 8, Urania, the Muse of Astronomy, from a tapestry border in *The Story of Rinaldo and Armida* cycle (designed by Simon Vouet, French, woven ca. 1633–37)

I would like to express my sincere gratitude to the Trustees of the Viola E. Bray Charitable Trust—Sally Ricker, William Ricker, Molly McCormick, and James Johnson—for their continuing operating support of the Viola E. Bray Gallery and for their support of this publication. Special thanks goes to the Whiting Foundation, and, for their generosity, to the Johnson Family, including Donald Johnson, Jr., Mary Alice Heaton, and Linda LeMieux, for continuing their parents' philanthropy and stewardship into the next generation. To Martha Piper and Robert Piper, I am deeply grateful for their enthusiasm and financial commitment of support for the project. I am also so grateful to the Isabel Foundation for their timely (2011) capital grant to create a gallery dedicated exclusively to decorative arts. This gallery will house additional objects contributed by Mrs. Bray, including extensive collections of eighteenth- and nineteenth-century European goblets and nineteenth- and twentieth-century European and American paperweights.

I would like to thank the National Endowment for the Arts for providing funds to support an associate curator position to research and write about the Bray collection. I am immensely grateful to Tracee Glab, who came to us from the Detroit Institute of Arts, where she served as editor of the museum's scholarly journal. Ms. Glab stepped into her new curatorial role with enthusiasm, applying her editorial and project coordination skills to the task of researching and writing about the collection, as well as overseeing many details of the project. Although some information existed for some objects, for most works there were only descriptions and outdated photographs in our files. The stylistic and artistic attributions and provenance information for almost all of these had been provided by French & Company to the FIA without any supporting documentation. Through her tenacious research, skillful communication, and unerring vision, Ms. Glab has succeeded in unraveling many of the mysteries that surrounded the collection, resulting in the remarkably cogent story that is told on the pages of this book. On behalf of everyone at the FIA, I wish to express my most sincere appreciation to the Charles Stewart Mott Foundation for their continued operating support, which has allowed the FIA to do "big things" over and above daily operations.

I am extremely grateful to all who contributed research to this project, starting with Charissa Bremer-David, Curator of Sculpture and Decorative Arts at the J. Paul Getty Museum, Los Angeles, California, whose contribution began with her first visit to the FIA in 2008, when she presented a lecture on Mrs. Bray and the tapestries. She remained interested in the project and revisited the tapestries in the summer of 2010 to continue her research. Ms. Bremer-David's initial observations and subsequent research on the origin and significance of the collection stimulated a more thorough examination of the meaning of the myriad characters and motifs, and the connections among them, that ultimately led to expanding the research and fund-raising for this publication.

Fig. 2. Detail of cat. 22b, female face on an andiron (Italian, late 16th c.)

In the initial planning stages, Duncan Cardillo, then Associate Curator at the FIA, was instrumental in conducting preliminary provenance research that was so useful later in obtaining funding for the project. The history of how these objects came together can be as fascinating as the objects themselves. Provenance research, therefore, has been an important and ongoing component of this project. Sale and auction catalogues were consulted, affirming previous ownership, as well as revealing heretofore unknown owners. Research on previous owners, including Florence Vanderbilt Twombly, Clarence Mackay, William Randolph Hearst, and William Payne Whitney, was also undertaken. French & Company stock records, currently at the J. Paul Getty Museum, were also obtained by Ms. Bremer-David after stock and negative numbers were gathered from the FIA curatorial files, with the assistance of Ms. Glab. Many stock sheets were found at the Getty, revealing new provenance information on several of the works. Arnauld Brejon de Lavergnée, Director of the Mobilier National et Manufactures des Gobelins in France, after hearing about this project from Ms. Bremer-David, offered to write an essay on Simon Vouet. We owe an enormous debt of gratitude to Mr. Brejon de Lavergnée for his dedicated research, which greatly enhanced this publication.

I wish to express my appreciation to others who helped discover hidden facts about the collection. Perhaps one of the most important discoveries was the result of correspondence with Alison Luchs, Curator at the National Gallery of Art, Washington, D.C., about the FIA's *Angels with Candlesticks* (cat. 15), attributed to Venetian sculptor Pietro Lombardo. Ms. Luchs, along with Matteo Ceriana, Director of the Accademia Gallery in Venice, and Anne Markham Schulz, Professor at Brown University, all agreed that these angels were by the hand of the Venetian architect and sculptor Giovanni Buora, working in the late fifteenth/early sixteenth century. Other research discoveries included finding a rare reference to Vincent Nanques, a French sculptor working in the seventeenth century. While his name is carved in the wooden sculpture of Mary Magdalene (cat. 20), little to nothing is known about him. That we now know his origin (Amiens) and the date of his marriage in Paris (1697) may possibly lead to more information about him in the future.

I would like to thank other scholars who offered advice or information about works in their collections that are similar to works in the Bray collection: Leticia Azcue, Senior Curator of Sculpture and Decorative Arts, Museo Nacional del Prado, Madrid, Spain; Pat Boulware, Collections Documentation Assistant, Saint Louis Art Museum; Antonia Boström, Curator, J. Paul Getty Museum, Los Angeles; Caryl Burtner, Coordinator of Curatorial Administration, Virginia Museum of Fine Arts; Guido Cornini, Curator, Vatican Museums; Sarah Cartwright, Research Associate, Robert Lehman Collection, Metropolitan Museum of Art, New York; Alan Darr, Curator of Sculpture and Decorative Arts, Detroit Institute of Arts; Catherine Futter, Curator of Decorative Arts at the Nelson-Atkins

Museum of Art, Kansas City, Missouri; Brian Gallagher, Curator of Decorative Arts, Mint Museum, Charlotte, North Carolina; Suzanne Higgott, Curator of Glass, Limoges Painted Enamels and Earthenwares, Wallace Collection, London; Tamara Schechter, Research Assistant, Department of European Sculpture and Decorative Arts, Metropolitan Museum of Art, New York; Dominique Vasseur, Curator of European Art, Columbus Museum of Art, Ohio; and Charlotte Vignon, Associate Curator of Decorative Arts, The Frick Collection, New York. I am also indebted to R. J. Kelly, III, for his insightful commentary, donation of scholarly materials, and translation services. Mr. James Ricker was also very helpful in providing information about Mrs. Bray.

This publication would not have been possible without the hard work and team effort of the FIA curatorial department, headed by Michael Martin, Coordinator of Collections and Exhibitions, and including Peter Ott, Assistant Registrar, and Heather Jackson, Assistant to the Registrar, who provided support and assistance throughout all stages of the project. Kathryn Sharbaugh, Assistant Director of Development, and Tracey Stewart, Development Officer, orchestrated fund-raising efforts; Monique Desormeau, Curator of Education, Judy Irwin, Director's Administrative Assistant, and Miles Lam, Senior Graphic Designer, also assisted the project in important ways. Outside of the museum, Mike Savitski of Savitski Design organized the graphic design details of the stunning book you hold in your hands; Stephen Robert Frankel carefully edited this work; and Monica Rumsey compiled the index. I would like to take this opportunity to express my debt of gratitude to Robert Hensleigh and Tim Thayer for their great achievement in producing the spectacular images on the pages that follow. Their high-resolution photographs, together with the new research provided herein, make it possible to study the collection in ways that were not imagined before.

John B. Henry, III
Director, Flint Institute of Arts

1   Mrs. William L. Richards formally dedicated the gallery on November 7, 1961 in memory of her mother, Viola E. Bray, and the opening to the public occurred on the following day; "The History of the First Five Years of the Founders Society of the Flint Institute of Arts," anonymous undated typescript, p. 101.

2   G. Stuart Hodge was FIA director from 1959 to 1980. The publication referred to here is not dated, but it is likely that it was published in 1963, according to the following information: The layout of the catalogue was approved by William Richards in a letter to G. Stuart Hodge dated August 16, 1963 (in FIA curatorial file 2005.158). The statement that 250 catalogues were mailed in 1963 to museums and galleries across the country appears in "The Flint Institute of Arts: 1928 to 1963," an anonymous undated typescript (referred to hereafter as "FIA 1928–63" typescript). The "FIA First Five Years" typescript (see preceding note) discusses the Bray gallery's grand opening on the 7 and 8 of November 1961 (p. 101) but does not mention the catalogue in its account of the years 1961 and 1962.

John B. Henry, III

The Viola E. Bray Gallery
in the Flint Institute of Arts

The Viola E. Bray Gallery at the Flint Institute of Arts and the exceptional objects within are frequently cited by museum visitors as their most memorable experience. The breathtaking design, scale, and decorative features of the gallery, so reminiscent of the *palazzos* of the Renaissance and Baroque eras, create a grand stage for the furniture and objects within and leave a lasting impression on all who visit. Donated by Mrs. Bray in 1961, the collection contains more than fifty works in various media. Among these works are the rare set of ten tapestries based on designs by Simon Vouet, first painter to Louis XIII of France; one of only two cutout panel paintings by Flemish artist Peter Paul Rubens; masterfully sculpted works in bronze, sandstone, and wood; exquisite vessels of maiolica (see fig. 1); and intricately carved furniture.

The visual power of the gallery's ten large tapestries is at once captivating and provocative: although their serial relationship is obvious, the stories they tell, at least for most visitors, are enigmatic and elusive. European works of art from the fifteenth through the seventeenth centuries often employed a special language of symbols that today are understood by almost no one except scholars. The Renaissance and Baroque works of art in the Viola E. Bray collection bear many of these symbols, and the relationship between the tapestries and the other objects is a clever compilation of decorative motifs and symbolism that require a viewer to have knowledge of the religious and mythological subjects represented in the images.

In the early 1630s, when the FIA tapestries were created, both the subject matter and how it was depicted would have been as familiar as action figures are to us today. Design elements in the tapestries, from the decorative foliage in the borders to the background architecture, carry layers of meaning to support and enhance the narrative. The symbols used were not new in the seventeenth century but had their origin in the fifteenth and sixteenth centuries, when artists and writers revived ancient visual and written sources to convey various ideas in works of all media, including paintings, tapestries, sculpture, furniture, decorative arts, poetry, and prose. Secular and sacred themes and references were often united by a common interest, which was shared throughout Europe, in reviving the ancient classical past of Greece and Rome. The Viola E. Bray Gallery offers a unique opportunity to study how these symbols migrated across borders and through time.

Identifying the central characters in the tapestries would have been easy for viewers in the early seventeenth century. The artist Simon Vouet and the Raphaël de La Planche

Fig. 1. Style of Fontana family, *Vase*, with *The Judgment of Paris*, late 16th century (cat. 13a)

Opposite: Fig. 2. Detail of cat. 9,
Fortitude, from a tapestry border
in *The Story of Rinaldo and Armida*
cycle (designed by Simon Vouet,
French, woven ca. 1633–37)

Above: Fig. 3. Detail of cat. 32,
cherub on a two-part cabinet
(French or Italian, 16th c.)

tapestry workshop followed descriptions in Torquato Tasso's widely known and popular poem *Gerusalemme Liberata* (*Jerusalem Delivered*) of 1581 (see translation of relevant verses in cats. 1–10 of this volume). Today, however, the characters in the poem are obscure, and the other figures and objects depicted in the tapestries' borders can be difficult to identify (see fig. 2). Symbolic images on other works in the Bray collection pose the same challenge (see fig. 3). For someone who has no knowledge of the story, the interrelationships among the symbols and their meaning are lost. Our research on this collection focused specifically on unraveling the mystery of each object to reveal its hidden meaning. We were surprised and delighted to discover an even deeper, more complex relationship among the objects, thanks to the intuitive curatorial pairing of the tapestries with the objects, by Mitchell Samuels, co-founder (with Percy W. French) of French & Company, the New York firm that sold the collection to Mrs. Bray.

History of the Bray Collection

In the late 1950s, when many American collectors were paying top dollar for works by Pablo Picasso[1] and the French Impressionists, Mrs. Bray looked to the more distant past for works to purchase. On Samuels's advice, Mrs. Bray decided to purchase items from this era "so that the ambience of a Renaissance hall would be fully achieved."[2] By 1958, she had purchased a total of forty-nine objects, all intended to be displayed together in a Renaissance setting. Later the next year, she acquired a complete set of seventeenth-century French tapestries. Although Mrs. Bray was an avid art collector and connoisseur, she did not purchase these particular works for her own enjoyment—in fact, she never lived with a single object from this collection. Instead, she planned all along to give these works to the people of Flint through the Bray Gallery.

The DeWaters Art Center was the FIA's new home in the recently conceived Cultural Center, which was inaugurated during Flint's centennial celebration (in honor of the city's incorporation in 1855). When the FIA was informed of her generous gift,[3] it was determined that, in order to accommodate such large pieces, a special addition to the DeWaters Art Center would need to be built, which Mrs. Bray also paid for. The FIA was an important part of this large complex created to serve as a home for the performing, literary, and visual arts; and the addition of this wing to the DeWaters Art Center greatly enhanced its offerings. According to one observer at the time of the opening, "The magnificence of the room . . . awed the spectators."[4]

When the Bray Gallery opened in 1961, the FIA's collecting at that time focused mostly on American and European works from the nineteenth and twentieth centuries; and Mrs. Bray's generous and well-rounded gift therefore filled a void in the collection. Among the highlights of her gift are the complete set of seventeenth-century French tapestries after designs by Simon Vouet (see cats. 1–10); the unique cutout panel painting of an angel by Peter Paul Rubens (see cat. 11); a sixteenth-century maiolica wine cistern by the Orazio Fontana family workshop in Urbino (see cat. 12); a pair of *Angels Holding Candlesticks* by Venetian Renaissance architect and sculptor Giovanni Buora (figs. 4, 5); as well as Italian Renaissance and Baroque tables, chairs, chests, and bronzes, French Renaissance furniture, and a Spanish seventeenth-century candlestick. Many of these objects also passed through famous American and European collections. Among the names that appear in the provenance history of these works are Twombly (Vanderbilt), Hearst, Whitney, Mackay, Volpi, and Rothschild.

Mrs. Bray died five months before the tapestries and other Renaissance objects were installed in her gallery at the FIA, but the way they are arranged today is similar to the way she saw them arranged in New York City by French & Company. In order to obtain a sense of how the pieces would look together, the dealer displayed them in a room with the look of a Renaissance hall (fig. 6). Aspects of this French & Company gallery, including the flat skylight spanning most of the length of the room, became the model for the Flint gallery; indeed, French & Company's Samuels corresponded with the architect of the Flint gallery, offering his advice on how the Flint gallery, which would include a high coffered ceiling and travertine marble floor, should look.[5]

French & Company, founded in 1907, eventually became one of the largest art dealerships in the world. From 1907 until 1959, when they closed their doors, they helped develop the European portions of the art collections of many wealthy Americans, including J. Paul Getty, William Randolph Hearst, the Vanderbilts, and the Rockefellers.[6] According to an unpublished manuscript in the FIA's curatorial files, Samuels "acted in an advisory capacity and as an art consultant," in the assemblage of the Bray collection, with the intention that it be given to the FIA.[7]

Although some changes have been made to the Bray Gallery in the last fifty years, it looks mostly as it did in 1961. One of the most dramatic changes was not to the room itself but rather to one of its key works, Rubens's *Angel* (fig. 7), which hangs above the mantelpiece. In this photograph, the painting is seen on a rectangular canvas (see fig. 6), which it retained until conservation analysis revealed that it was originally on a shaped wooden panel conforming to the contours of the angel's body and drapery (see pp. 86–89 for more information on this discovery). It was decided, after thorough research and discussion, that the painting should be restored to its original shape, which is how it is displayed today. Other changes to the gallery include the addition of platforms to showcase the works, improved lighting to protect the tapestries, and the inclusion of didactic labels. Mrs. Bray did not live to see her gift realized, but today her legacy lives on through the Bray Charitable Trust.[8]

Fig. 6. Photograph of French & Company gallery, New York City, with Rubens's *Angel* above the mantelpiece, ca. 1950s. Research Library, The Getty Research Institute, Los Angeles (97.P.7). Photo © J. Paul Getty Trust

Fig. 7. Peter Paul Rubens (1577–1640), *Angel*, 1610/11 (cat. 11)

Viola Estella Bray

The Viola E. Bray Gallery in the Flint Institute of Arts demonstrates not only an exciting period of our city's history, when the arts were infused with a vital awareness of the past and the present, but also the vision of a unique and generous woman. Mrs. Bray's gift of these works of art, and the special gallery in which to exhibit them, reflects both her beneficence and her passion for history. An avid art collector, she not only acquired beautiful works but also studied them closely as a way to gain insight into the past. Mrs. Bray (figs. 8, 9) chose to share her enthusiasm for art and history with the community in which she lived and worked by establishing the Viola E. Bray Gallery, with its fifty-plus Renaissance and Baroque works of art, and the Bray Charitable Trust, providing funds for the care and maintenance of the collection (such as the restoration of the Rubens), the acquisition of new works, and other cultural endeavors.

What do we know about her personal history? She was born on March 5, 1873, in Flushing, Michigan, to Sally (Wiggins) Swart and Menzo Swart, a Union officer in the Civil War. The Swart family moved to Flint in 1879. Viola graduated from the Flint Union High School, then attended Olivet College in Olivet, Michigan. She was a schoolteacher before her marriage, in 1902, to Everett Lewis Bray (1864–1935), a Flint lawyer. Everett's connection to Flint began when his maternal grandparents, Daniel and Julia Seeley, moved to the area at a time when only seven houses had been built there, on the site of a fur-trading post established in 1819. In 1908, Everett Bray served as one of the legal aides in the reorganization of the Buick Motor Company, which led to the foundation of General Motors, headed by William C. Durant. The Brays had one daughter, Bertha, who married William L. Richards, and they had a daughter, Sally (who married and is now Sally Richards Ricker). After Everett's death in 1935, Viola continued to live in Flint, participating in several local groups that supported the arts and a number of patriotic and historical societies. At various times she was involved with the Daughters of the American Revolution, the Daughters of American Colonists, the Daughters of Founders and Patriots of America, the Daughters of Colonial Wars, the Colonial Dames of America, the Huguenot Society of Michigan, and the Art Class of Flint.

In addition to her social and community groups, Mrs. Bray spent much time researching her family's history, eventually writing and publishing a book on the Bray, Swart, and allied families.[9] Her research skills and desire for knowledge carried over to her collecting practices. She loved to research and record everything there was to know about the works she acquired. According to those close to her, she had a very keen mind, and was always ready with a historical fact or anecdote about a work in her collection.[10] One person wrote of Mrs. Bray: "A woman of exquisite taste, she brought an extensive knowledge to the project which, combined with her enthusiasm, makes an ideal collector."[11] She especially admired paperweights and works of glass, collecting hundreds of fine examples, many of which are now in the FIA collection (given by her daughter and son-in-law). Her travels to the East Coast and Europe gave her opportunities to collect items said to have once been owned by Louis XV's queen consort, Marie Leszczyńska, and Lucy, Countess of Egmont (purportedly an ancestor of Mrs. Bray). It was on one of her travels east that she visited French & Company in New York City, where she purchased the set of ten French tapestries that would become the centerpiece of the collection she donated to the FIA.

Viola Bray died on May 24, 1961. However, her memory lives on in her collection and in the gallery she established, and the Bray Charitable Trust continues to care for that precious collection of art, which she gave to the people of Flint.

1 A November 1958 auction set a record price paid for Picasso's painting *Mother and Child* (1903) when it sold for $152,000; Aline B. Saarinen, "Auction of Art Brings $1,548,500," New York Times November 20, 1958, p. 1.
2 Foreword by G. Stuart Hodge, in Flint 1963, n.p.
3 The Bray collection, though in the custody of the FIA, was owned by the Flint Board of Education until 2005, when the works were officially accessioned by the FIA.
4 "FIA 1928–63" typescript, p. 101.
5 Charissa Bremer-David, e-mail to Tracee Glab, May 2, 2010.

6 The French & Company archives and records are now located at the Getty Research Institute. See Charissa Bremer-David, "Building American Collections of European Tapestries: The Role & Influence of French & Company," lecture at the Minneapolis Institute of Arts, May 9, 2002, pdf. file accessed at http://tapestrycenter.org/wp-content/uploads/2008/12/4th-annual-lecture-bremer-david-transcript1.pdf.
7 "The Bray Collection," anonymous undated typescript (FIA curatorial file 2005.124). Although this manuscript is undated, it must be from 1958 or later, as it bears French & Company's 980 Madison Avenue, New York City address, to which the firm moved in 1958 from their old premises on E. 57th Street.

8 Mrs. Bray left a trust fund of 30,000 shares of General Motors stock; "FIA 1928–63" typescript, p. 102. In 1961, at $45 a share, they were worth $1.35 million.
9 See Viola E. Bray, *Bray-Swart and Allied Families* (New York: The American Historical Company, 1941).
10 James Ricker, conversation with Tracee Glab, April 8, 2010.
11 FIA, Anonymous, "The Bray Collection," typed manuscript (see note 7 above), FIA curatorial file, 2005.124; undated.

Tracee J. Glab

Decoding Renaissance and Baroque Symbols in the Bray Collection

The enthusiastic reception of Dan Brown's novel *The Da Vinci Code*, which deciphered symbols in the art of Renaissance master Leonardo da Vinci, demonstrates the public's desire to know how to "read" art, especially the complex symbols of the distant past. Although *The Da Vinci Code* is a work of fiction, it is true that significant elements of most Renaissance and Baroque works of art are based on special codes that are obscure to many today, except scholars. For example, what are wrestling satyrs doing on a tapestry about a love story set during the First Christian Crusade (fig. 1)? Why do disembodied faces and fantastical creatures appear on the surfaces of decorative arts (figs. 2, 3)?

These questions and more like them may occur to the twenty-first-century visitor to the Viola E. Bray Gallery at the Flint Institute of Arts. In this single gallery, a panoply of different figures, symbols, and motifs are depicted on the Renaissance and Baroque works of art, including tapestries, furniture, sculpture, and other decorative arts. Many of these images have, in a sense, lost their meaning to us today because we are no longer familiar with the stories and ideas that they represent. However, some of this meaning could be recovered if we were able to understand the symbols and their origins. The purpose of this essay is to provide the viewer with some tools to "decode" these symbols in order to gain a richer visual and emotional experience and to find the similarities, concordances, and relationships among seemingly disparate works of art.

Opposite: Fig. 1. Detail of cat. 2, satyrs wrestling, from a tapestry border in *The Story of Rinaldo and Armida* cycle (designed by Simon Vouet, French, woven ca. 1633–37)

From left to right: Fig. 2. Detail of cat. 23, face on a mantelpiece (French, 16th c.)

Fig. 3. Detail of cat. 12, fantastical creatures on a wine cistern (workshop of Orazio Fontana, Italian, 1565–75)

Fig. 4. Harry Peter, cover of *Wonder Woman*, issue #1, summer 1942, showing Wonder Woman leading the U.S. cavalry against the Nazis. Wonder Woman is ™ and © DC Comics

One must be careful assigning meaning to symbols when interpreting such works centuries after they were originally made and, moreover, addressing an audience completely different from the one for whom the objects were created. Even if there are primary or contemporary sources available to consult, it is not always clear what the symbols in a work specifically mean. Complicating things even further, a single symbol in a single work could have multiple meanings. To grasp how the meaning of symbols can change over time, even when there might have been an agreed-upon meaning originally, imagine how the image of a comic-book hero would be interpreted four hundred years in the future. How would a twenty-sixth-century person interpret the twentieth-century depiction of a white woman wearing a red-and-blue star-spangled outfit, adorned with a golden rope, bracelets, and tiara (fig. 4)? Even if that person in the future understood that the woman was meant to be an Amazon (the female warrior of Greek mythology), he or she would probably not recognize the figure as Wonder Woman, the first DC Comics superheroine. This character, created in the United States in 1941, reveals more about American culture during that period than about her Greek mythological origins. And, even in the seventy years since she was created, her image (and meaning) has changed to reflect current cultural concerns. So, when we trace images and ideas back to the past, we must always carefully consider them in terms of their original setting as much as possible, concerning both medium and context.[1]

Determining a symbol's context, as well as any primary source material that might help explain it, is vital. To use our comic-book heroine as an example, the future researcher would be able to obtain more cogent information about the symbols involved if he or she understood Wonder Woman's appearance in a comic-book format rather than in a religious, government, or domestic setting. The text accompanying the image would also tell the researcher more about what she meant to that audience. In terms of the works in the Bray collection, many of them were created for household or domestic settings, others for a religious context. Some of the works also have texts associated with them, which can further our understanding of the original meaning of the image.

In our fictional future, Wonder Woman would need to be "translated" in order to be interpreted; but today, to most viewers in an American audience at least, her identity is well understood, even if the viewer has never read any of the comic books devoted to her adventures. Her appearance in television shows, video games, and animated films decades after her debut in DC Comics has made her image even more widespread, and her status as a superheroine gives her a certain identifiable meaning, even if a viewer does not know the specific meaning of her attributes (e.g., identifying the golden lasso as the Lasso of Truth) or understand her Greek mythological origins (the all-female Amazon warriors). The more one knows about the source, context, and texts surrounding a symbol, the easier it is to interpret and understand the image and its message.

For works in the Bray collection, created so long ago, accessibility to the meaning of the images is not assured. Art historians and museum curators have done research to understand these symbols, but even they have not found all the answers, especially if no text or reproduced images exist to explicate the various meanings. For viewers in the Renaissance and Baroque periods, this system of symbols would have been much more accessible than to us today, and for this reason these symbols have been called a type of international language in the textual and visual arts.[2] This does not necessarily mean that the symbols' meanings were understood by everyone during those periods, as the appearance and communication of these images also depended on one's class, education, gender, race, and religion.

Commonalities and understandings did exist among erudite people, or those "in the know," that would have been lost to outsiders—a code often deliberately employed to keep some knowledge secret. During the fifteenth and sixteenth centuries, the allure of many symbols to that elite group was the fact that they could not be interpreted or understood by the majority of people. Egyptian hieroglyphs, for example, fascinated Renaissance humanists who considered this pictorial writing to be a lost divine language or the *priscorum theologia* (theology of the ancients).[3] Before the Rosetta Stone was discovered in 1799 and translated in 1822, hieroglyphs were not understood at all, but writers during the Renaissance period decided that these ancient symbols must represent divine wisdom.

Symbols deriving from ancient Greek and Roman texts and images were also embraced because of their mysterious nature, having meaning for just an initiated few. Some even thought that divine wisdom could only be received if communicated through a veiled medium.[4] For example, Giovanni Pico della Mirandola, a fifteenth-century Italian philosopher, wrote that the Greek myths revealed "only the crust of the mysteries to the vulgar, while reserving the marrow of the true sense for higher and more perfect spirits."[5]

Renaissance and Baroque viewers were fascinated by the ancient Greek and Roman periods. Their interest in ancient cultures had its origins in the early medieval period,

beginning in the fourth century, when Christians and pagans coexisted in the Roman Empire. Representations of pagan gods and ideas were often appropriated by Christians, imbued with a new meaning, but still carrying within it similarities to the original image— such as artists using the image of the Greek sun god Helios to depict Jesus Christ, as he was the Son of God.[6] Pagan images continued to persist throughout the Middle Ages, changed to reflect Christian meaning as needed.[7] Therefore, when Renaissance artists depicted images of the past, they were often more familiar with the medieval version of these depictions than with the original classical source.[8]

Indeed, the Christian images and ideas also carried the same type of mysterious connotations that the pagan images did. Looking to the Hebrew Bible (the Old Testament), Renaissance scholars considered it to be another type of hidden divine wisdom. Some even postulated that these various texts, from Greek mythology to Mosaic Law, were all divine revelations.[9] Writers and artists in the Middle Ages also continued a legacy of allegory, where one could interpret a person from history, the Old Testament, or mythology as being a type of Christ, as well as use pagan images to communicate Christian thought.[10]

Even though images from the ancient Greek and Roman periods had survived during the Middle Ages, people during the Renaissance embraced them in radically different ways by studying or "rediscovering" the original source material.[11] As early as the fourteenth century, writers Petrarch and Boccaccio advocated the study of Greek language and culture.[12] In the fifteenth century, many Renaissance figures, including Pope Paul II and sculptor Lorenzo Ghiberti, collected antiquities, including coins, gems, and statues.[13] One of the first depictions in the Renaissance of a mythological subject on a large scale was Sandro Botticelli's painting *The Birth of Venus* in the 1480s (fig. 5).[14]

In addition to the rediscovery of known classical texts and artworks, important ancient objects were unearthed during the fifteenth century. In Rome, the underground ruins of Nero's *Domus Aurea* (Golden Palace), built after AD 64, were discovered and excavated in the 1480s, and contained intact painted surfaces (fig. 6). Those who descended into the

Fig. 6. Painted decoration in one
of the rooms in the *Domus Aurea*
(Golden Palace) of Nero, Palatine
Hill, Rome. Photo: Werner Forman/
Art Resource, NY

grotto, or cave, found fantastical creatures and hybrid figures depicted as wall decoration.
Artists who visited the site made sketches of the images, which became known as *grotteschi*
(grotesques),[15] and these sketches inspired other artists, including Pinturicchio and Raphael,
thus initiating a style that would be used for many generations. Other works, such as the
famous ancient Greek sculpture *Laocoön and His Sons* (discovered in 1506), inspired artists,
even causing a demand for fakes among collectors.[16] Artists not only copied these ancient
examples to perfect form and style but also studied the relevant texts to understand how to
represent something truly classical.[17] Throughout the sixteenth and seventeenth centuries,
this trend continued, with artists continuing to study ancient art and literature, and
expressing the classical tradition in their own style.

Renaissance artists not only tried to emulate the style and ideas of the classical
period, but also wanted to capture some of the symbolic meanings of art from the
past. In didactic illustrated books known as emblem books, such as Andrea Alciati's
Emblematum Liber (1531), images were accompanied by an *inscription* (terse motto)
and a *subscription* (statement below the picture). Emblems were meant to communicate
a moral lesson or truth, but the meaning was usually ambiguous and required the viewer
to use his or her intellect to provide an interpretation.[18] These emblem books were
popular among the *cognoscenti*, with more than five thousand versions by the end of
the eighteenth century.[19] Because of the emblem's enigmatic formula and the variety
of interpretations, many of these images are often misunderstood today, largely because
we no longer share the same knowledge.[20]

Another contemporary work, Cesare Ripa's *Iconologia* (1593), offers some insight into
the popularity of coded symbols. First composed strictly of text, with images added later in
1603, this work was a guide to the symbolism in emblem books and became an important
source for representing allegories (abstract ideas depicted in figural form). Ripa used ancient
sources, such as works by Aristotle, Ovid, Homer, and Pliny, but also appropriated medieval
texts, such as bestiaries (books that described the traits of various real and mythical animals)

to depict such abstract ideas as innocence, sin, confusion, strength, fear, and hope, among many others.[21]

The works in the Bray collection also reflect this fascination with symbols derived from ancient Greek and Roman art. Because symbols sometimes have more than one meaning, it is often difficult to group them by theme or subject; but I have attempted here to organize the symbols found in these works under five thematic headings, preceded by an introductory section, "Looking to the Past," which examines how these depictions of classical figures and ornamentation suggested the atmosphere of the ancient world. Deriving from the common idea of reviving the past, the following themes are examined in the context of various works in the Bray collection: Power and Status, Wisdom and Secret Knowledge, Love and Lust, Faith and Virtue, and Abundance and Fruitfulness.

Looking to the Past

Images that had their origin in ancient Greek and Roman art were used in Renaissance and Baroque art and decorative objects in a variety of ways to suggest the owner's wealth, power, and wisdom or to evoke attributes of love, faith, or virtue. Often, these images were used to create what one writer called a "dreamworld of antiquity" rather than to suggest a specific meaning.[22] Faces lurk in many places in the Bray collection as profiles or masks, decorative devices imparting an ancient flavor to these works of the sixteenth

and seventeenth centuries. The male and female heads in profile on the sides of the mantelpiece (figs. 7, 8), for example, are derived from the style of ancient Roman cameos. Other faces (as in some of the ceramic objects, cats. 12, 13, and carved wood furniture, cats. 32, 34, and 35) had their inspiration in grotesques, which contained faces, masks, and human figures usually among animals, birds, foliage, fruit, fantastical creatures, and architectural devices (see figs. 9, 10). This ancient Roman style of ornament (see fig. 6) captured the imaginations of Renaissance artists and viewers alike, with one contemporary writing, "If you have time, allow yourself to be taken to the grotesques underground and you will see the grandeur of the ancients."[23] Frequently, as has been pointed out, the use of this ancient style on furniture and other decorative arts was appreciated because of its fantastical and playful nature rather than for any strict literal meaning.[24]

Another type of antique ornament employed on tapestries, furniture, and decorative arts, called the *maniera all'antica* (decoration in the ancient manner, or in the style of antiquity), imitates or quotes the vocabulary of classical architecture. Artists applied the Greek style of Corinthian, Doric, or Ionic columns, known as the classical orders, in these works to instantly communicate the idea of a distant time and place. For example, in one of the ten tapestries depicting the *Story of Rinaldo and Armida* (fig. 11 and cat. 5, where Carlo and Ubaldo are shown spying on Rinaldo and Armida), the design includes images of classical architecture depicting Armida's palace in the background. Another tapestry panel, "Carlo and Ubaldo at the Fountain of Laughter" (cat. 4), includes an element of classical architecture that is related to decorative ornaments elsewhere in the Bray gallery: a telamon (a support sculpted in the form of a male figure, used in place of a column or pier) behind the nymphs in the water as part of the architecture framing the fountain, along with a dolphin and a putto. Closely associated with this architectural device are the herms (pillar figures also known as terms) used on a *credenza* and two-part cabinet (cats. 26 and 31).[25]

Other aspects of classical architecture visible on the furniture in the Bray gallery are egg-and-dart molding, roundels, scrollwork, and bead-and-reel molding (see cats. 27

Fig. 12. Detail of cat. 24a, festoon on a *cassone* (Italian, 16th c.)

Fig. 13. Detail of cat. 30, lion's–paw feet on a table (Italian, 15th c.)

and 40, for example). *All'antica* decoration also includes organic motifs, with acanthus leaves, palmettes, rinceaux, garlands, and wreaths serving as essential parts of the ornamentation. An ancient story associating acanthus leaves with life arising from death could also imply rebirth and renewal.[26] The swirling vinelike ornamentation known as rinceaux (prominently depicted on the tapestry borders) was inspired by the branches and vines seen in ancient ruins. Swags of fruits and flowers, also known as festoons, could be seen on ancient Roman stone sarcophagi or altars, carved to mimic the real festoons used during commemorative occasions. The occasion that led to the carving of festoons on the pair of sixteenth-century *cassoni* (fig. 12) was most likely the celebration of a wedding.

Animal motifs were also typical elements of antique ornamentation, with images of dolphins, lions, and eagles, offering artists a system of visual shorthand to evoke an ancient setting. One such motif, lion's-paw feet (fig. 13), was frequently employed in Renaissance furniture; derived from ancient counterparts, this may have indicated an object's portability.

Power and Status

Symbols of power, strength, and status used on some of the objects in the Bray collection are closely related to the narrative that is depicted on those pieces. On the tapestries, for example, the Roman god of war, Mars, is featured in some of the cartouches (cats. 1, 6, 7, and 9) as a reference to one of the two main characters in the tapestries' narrative, the Christian knight Rinaldo, who fought the Saracens during the First Crusade (fig. 14). However, the way Mars is shown in these cartouches, in a reclining pose with the weapons of war at his feet (i.e., in love rather than at war), refers more to his relationship with Venus, the goddess of love (see "Love and Lust" below) and thus relates more to the overt narrative of Rinaldo and Armida's love affair.[27] Depictions of Mars in sixteenth-century allegories of Peace also show him reclining, with one hand supporting his head, apparently asleep.[28] One of Mars's attributes is the ram, seen on the prow of the Christian knights' boat (fig. 15) and on the lower cartouches of the tapestries (cats. 1–10). On the maiolica wine cistern (cat. 12), featuring a naval battle scene in the interior of the basin, the warlike and powerful aspect of Mars is referenced by the military weapons and trophies depicted on the rim.[29]

Symbols derived from the animal kingdom have also been used to portray power and status. The lion as a symbol of power was one of the most effective symbols because of the many beliefs associated with him—for example, that the lion did not fear any other animal

and did not hide from hunters;[30] that he never forgot an insult, waiting for the perfect opportunity to take revenge on his enemies;[31] and that he slept with his eyes open, thus becoming associated with watchfulness and guardianship.[32] In addition to power and strength, the lion was considered the most noble of the beasts, ranking higher than all the others. This animal appears in the form of heads or masks on the Bray collection's wine cistern and one of the pair of vases (cats. 12 and 13) and on its pair of andirons, its *cassoni*, its *credenza*, and one of the two-part cabinets (cats. 24, 26, and 31; fig. 16). Another ancient symbol of power was the eagle, sacred to Jupiter, the ruler of the gods; eagles were depicted on the standards of ancient Roman legions. In the Bray collection, they appear as symbols of power in the pair of andirons (fig. 17) and on several pieces of furniture (cats. 24, 25, and 31). Christians also used the symbol of the eagle as the attribute of John the Evangelist.[33]

Wisdom and Secret Knowledge

The mere presence of a symbol on a work of art could suggest wisdom and knowledge, which were often a prerequisite for a viewer to understand its meaning. Wisdom has frequently been represented by specific figures from mythology. In Greek myth, Athena, the goddess of war and wisdom, sprang fully formed from the head of Zeus, her father. In Roman myth, she was known as Minerva and became the personification of wisdom, often shown with an owl perched on a pile of books.[34] In some of the cartouches on the Bray

collection's tapestries and on the door of the two-part cabinet (cats. 2, 5, and 31; fig. 18),
she is shown only with her weapons, but she could have been depicted to suggest both
interpretations. Minerva was also a patroness of the arts, learning, and crafts (including
weaving).[35] Minerva is often depicted with the following attributes: helmet (with sphinx),
shield with the face of Medusa (a Gorgon defeated by the hero Perseus), and spear. The
sphinx at the top of her helmet, which is shown isolated above the lower cartouches on all
the tapestries (fig. 19), was symbolic of secret knowledge. The sphinx had a woman's head
and breasts, a lion's body, wings, and a serpent's tail. Believed in antiquity to possess hidden
knowledge, she would kill anyone who could not answer her riddles. In Greek mythology,
Oedipus, the king of Thebes, conquered the sphinx by guessing the riddle she asked him,
which led her to take her own life in despair.[36] This aspect of the sphinx may be alluded to
in the tapestry panel "Rinaldo Prevents the Suicide of the Despairing Armida" (cat. 10).

Another god associated with wisdom is the messenger of the gods, Mercury (the
counterpart of the Greek god Hermes), shown with winged feet and helmet, and often
carrying a caduceus, a wand with two snakes entwining it (as in the cartouches on cats. 2
and 5; fig. 20). Considered a mediator between humans and the gods, he escorted departed
souls to Charon, the ferryman of Hades, the Greek underworld. As a mediator, he was
considered a patron of travelers but became associated with secret, mystical, or "hermetic"
knowledge.[37] Mercury is most likely depicted on those tapestry cartouches in his role as
patron of travelers (since Rinaldo and his companions are traveling in foreign lands); and
although Mercury is not shown in the tapestry depicting Armida summoning her magical
powers to enact her revenge on Rinaldo for abandoning her (cat. 8), he could nevertheless
be associated with those powers.

In the cartouches on other tapestries, two of the nine Muses are depicted: Calliope, the
Muse of Epic Poetry, has the attributes of trumpet, laurel crown, and writing instruments
(cats. 1, 6, 7, and 10); and Urania, the Muse of Astronomy, is shown with globe or armillary
sphere, compasses, and sometimes a circle of stars as a crown (cats. 4, 6, 8, and 10).[38] The
Muses, the offspring of Jupiter and Mnemosyne (Memory), who slept together for nine
nights, were considered to be the inspiration for creative works such as poetry, song, and
the arts. The other Muses are Clio (history), Euterpe (music), Thalia (comedy), Melpomene
(tragedy), Terpsichore (dancing and song), Erato (lyric and love poetry), and Polyhymnia
(heroic hymns).

Top left: Fig. 21. Detail of cat. 5,
Venus's attributes: roses, pearls,
and putti, from "Carlo and Ubaldo
Spy on the Lovers" in *The Story of
Rinaldo and Armida* tapestry cycle

Top right: Fig. 22. Detail of cat.
25a, Venus pulled in a water
chariot by swans on a parcel-
gilded cabinet (Italian, 17th c.)

Bottom: Fig. 23. Detail of cat. 4,
nymphs bathing in a fountain,
from "Carlo and Ubaldo at the
Fountain of Laughter" in *The
Story of Rinaldo and Armida*
tapestry cycle

Love and Lust

One of the most recognizable symbols of love and lust to sixteenth- and seventeenth-century viewers would have been Venus, the goddess of love. Venus (and her Greek counterpart, Aphrodite) had a long visual tradition that imbued her with many attributes and meanings.[39] Depicted as a beautiful, youthful woman, often nude, she was also accompanied by a variety of flora and fauna, which, when shown alone, also suggested the love goddess. Roses, for example, became a symbol of Venus, as it was said that she cut her foot on a rose thorn while running to defend her lover. The red petals on the rose were said to be derived from her blood.[40] Shells and pearls were also regarded as her attributes because of the myth that she was born fully formed in the ocean, riding to the shore on a shell (see fig. 5).[41] Although the figure of Venus is not depicted on the tapestries, her presence is suggested by the roses and pearls that appear in several panels (as in cat. 5; fig. 21). Other attributes of Venus include swans and doves, which came to symbolize love and faithfulness.[42] In the fifteenth century, Venus was seen as representing two kinds of love, celestial and earthly. Celestial love represented god and eternal things, while earthly love was preoccupied with the baser, everyday world[43] (as depicted in cat. 25; fig. 22). Venus's son Cupid was also associated with love and lust in the Renaissance and Baroque periods. Depicted as a child, usually with wings, Cupid is shown carrying a bow and arrow with which to shoot darts of love into the hearts of humankind[44] (as in cat. 1); and in one of the other tapestries, he is shown punishing Armida with whips made from strings of pearls (cat. 9).

While Venus could be depicted as representing either celestial or earthly love, other images could only be regarded as representing lust. Nymphs, often shown attending Venus, are nature spirits who were said to tempt mortals with their youth and beauty[45] (as in the tapestry "Carlo and Ubaldo at the Fountain of Laughter," cat. 4; fig. 23). Sirens, half women, half fish, similar to mermaids (see cat. 6), seduced men with their song.[46] And satyrs—half man, half goat—were said to constantly look for opportunities to have sex[47] (see fig. 1, and also in the lower corners of cats. 1, 2, 4–7, and 10). In Ripa's *Iconologia*, the personification of debauchery is a naked satyr with a wreath of vine leaves.[48] Another symbol that could represent the more passionate side of love was the horse, which must be tamed or bridled to curtail its lust[49] (horses pull Armida's chariot, as in cats. 2 and 3).

From left to right: Fig. 24. Detail of cat. 25a, Fortitude on a parcel-gilded cabinet (Italian, 17th c.)

Fig. 25. Detail of cat. 8, Prudence, from a tapestry border in *The Story of Rinaldo and Armida* cycle

Fig. 26. Detail of cat. 13b, Justice on a vase (style of Fontana family, Italian, late 16th c.)

Faith and Virtue

Other symbols used on objects in the Bray collection represent ideals of faith and virtue, often an allegorical figure, usually depicted as a woman. Three of the four Cardinal Virtues are represented on the tapestries by such figures: Fortitude, Prudence, and Justice (Temperance, the fourth, is not). Fortitude, which symbolizes courage and strength, is shown with a column or pillar, derived from the biblical account of Samson pulling down the columns of the Philistine palace with his bare hands[50] (as in border cartouches in cats. 1, 3, 7, and 9). An image of Fortitude is also included on the parcel-gilded cabinet (fig. 24). Prudence, which signifies wise behavior, is depicted with a snake and mirror (see cats. 3, 4, 8, and 10; fig. 25). The snake refers to a passage from the New Testament: "Be ye wise (*prudentes*) as serpents" (Matthew 10:16), while the mirror refers to being able to see yourself as you really are;[51] a mirror is featured even more prominently in the central panel of "Rinaldo Views His Image in the Diamond Shield" (cat. 6). Justice is shown with scales, to measure things accurately, and a sword, to mete out punishment to those who deserve it (see cats. 1, 2, 5, 6, and 13; fig. 26).[52]

Other symbols of faith and virtue include the anchor, skull, shell, sunflower, and palm leaf. The anchor, often depicted with the allegorical figure of Hope, implies the immovability of faith in the midst of a stormy life (part of an anchor can be seen with Fortitude in cat. 25).[53] The skull, a traditional *memento mori*, suggests that faith and repentance of sins come from remembering that we are all bound for the grave[54] (see the use of a skull in the depiction of Mary Magdalene in cat. 20). The shell, which has also been associated with the goddess of love, Venus, was later appropriated by Christians to represent a pilgrimage, a sacred journey to churches and shrines that held relics of martyr saints.[55] The sunflower was another pagan symbol turned Christian (see cat. 2). According to myth, Clytie turned into a sunflower while pining after the sun-god Apollo; later, that flower came to represent a Christian believer, dependent on the Son of God for guidance: just as the sunflower would follow the sun, so too would the faithful soul.[56] Palm leaves represent faith and virtue in their association with the palm tree, which is strong and immovable during harsh storms. Palm leaves were used in victor's wreaths and crowns, and were later shown in depictions of Christian martyrs as a symbol of their heavenly reward and victory over death (see cat. 16).[57] Another prominent symbol of Christian faith in the Bray collection is the figure of an angel (see cats. 11, 15, and 17). These supernatural beings, who were

Top, left to right: Fig. 27. Detail of cat. 31, swag of fruit on drawer front of a two-part cabinet (French or Italian, 16th c.)

Above: Fig. 30. Detail of cat. 28, cornucopia and spiraled snake on legs of a table (Italian, 16th c.)

Fig. 28. Detail of cat. 3, cluster of fruit with pomegranate, from a tapestry border in *The Story of Rinaldo and Armida* cycle

Fig. 29. Detail of cat. 24b, putto with cornucopia on a *cassone* (Italian, 16th c.)

messengers of God and agents of his will on earth, are usually depicted as gender-neutral, sometimes with wings and clothed in drapery. In Baroque art, they are often shown as winged infants known as putti (see tapestry borders, cats. 1–10).[58]

Abundance and Fruitfulness

Some of the symbols on works in the Bray collection were probably included to represent the owners' desire for an abundant and fruitful life. Many of these symbols are derived from the natural world, including trees, flowers, and fruit (see figs. 27–29). One that is frequently depicted is the pomegranate. This fruit was symbolic of unity and concord, as a single pomegranate contains hundreds of seeds.[59] This abundance of seeds was also associated with fertility and fruitfulness (the notion that many can come from one). In a Christian context, it was a symbol of Christ's Resurrection, because of the ancient myth of Persephone.[60] According to myth, Persephone was abducted by Hades, god of the underworld, to be his wife. Her mother Ceres, goddess of the earth, protested this marriage to the gods, who agreed that Persephone should be returned. Just as Persephone was about to be released, however, she was offered a pomegranate by Hades. She accepted one bite and, as a result, was consigned to live in the darkness of the underworld with her husband Hades six months of every year. Persephone's absence from her mother for half the year accounts for fall and winter, while her return (or resurrection from the earth) heralds the spring and summer months.

The attributes of Ceres also can be found on several works in the Bray collection. As Roman goddess of the earth and agriculture, she is linked with the bounty of the earth, including wheat and corn. She was also associated with snakes, which in ancient Greece were not seen as evil but linked to fertility, as they came up out of the ground.[61] The cornucopia, which literally means "horn of plenty," was also an attribute of Ceres. According to ancient belief, power and fertility were found in a goat's or bull's horn. The cornucopia—a horn shown overflowing with vegetables, fruit, or shafts of wheat— symbolized abundance (as in cats. 28 and 29; fig. 30). In emblem books where the attributes of Joy, Abundance, and Peace are depicted, a frequent motif used to represent those virtues is the cornucopia—the ultimate symbol of a full and carefree life.[62]

My thanks to R. J. Kelly, III for his helpful comments and suggestions, as well as for providing research material. I also wish to thank Stephen Robert Frankel for his insightful editing.

1   On the problem of misconceptions in interpreting the meaning of images and ideas from earlier times, see E. H. Gombrich, *Symbolic Images: Studies in the Art of the Renaissance*, 2nd ed. (London: Phaidon 1978), p. 2, where he discusses the statue of Eros in Piccadilly Square, London.

2   See Edward A. Maser, "Introduction," in Cesare Ripa, *Baroque and Rococo Pictorial Imagery: The 1758–60 Hertel Edition of Ripa's* Iconologia *with 200 Engraved Illustrations*, ed. Edward A. Maser (New York: Dover, 1971), p. vii.

3   See John F. Moffitt, "Introduction," in Andrea Alciati, *A Book of Emblems: The* Emblematum Liber *in Latin and English*, trans. and ed. John F. Moffitt (Jefferson, N.C.: McFarland, 2004), p. 6.

4   Edgar Wind, *Pagan Mysteries in the Renaissance* (New York: Norton, 1968), p. 25.

5   Giovanni Pico della Mirandola, *Commento sopra una canzona de amore composta da Girolamo Beniveni* III, xi, 9, quoted in ibid., p. 17.

6   For example, the Christ/Helios mosaic in the tomb of the Julii, 3rd century, under St. Peter's Basilica, Vatican.

7   Erwin Panofsky, *Studies in Iconology: Humanistic Themes in the Art of the Renaissance* (New York: Harper & Row, 1972 paperback edition), pp. 69–70.

8   Ibid., p. 37.

9   Wind, *Pagan Mysteries*, p. 20.

10 Moffit, "Introduction," in Alciati, *A Book of Emblems*, p. 5.

11 Panofsky, *Studies in Iconology*, p. 18.

12 Wendy Stedman Sheard, *Antiquity in the Renaissance*, vol. 2, exh. cat. (Northampton, Mass.: Smith College Museum of Art, 1978), n.p.

13 John T. Paoletti and Gary M. Radke, *Art in Renaissance Italy* (Upper Saddle River, N.J.: Prentice Hall, 1997 paperback edition), 285; see also Roberto Weiss, *The Renaissance Discovery of Classical Antiquity*, 2nd ed. (Oxford: Basil Blackwell, 1988), pp. 180–202.

14 Ibid., p. 281.

15 For a discussion of *grotteschi*, see Nicole Dacos, *The Loggia of Raphael: A Vatican Art Treasure*, trans. Josephine Bacon (New York: Abbeville Press, 2008), p. 29.

16 Paoletti and Radke, *Art in Renaissance Italy*, p. 285.

17 Wind, *Pagan Mysteries*, p. 153.

18 Moffitt, "Introduction," in Alciati, *A Book of Emblems*, pp. 7–8.

19 Ibid., p. 10.

20 Charles Moseley, *A Century of Emblems: An Introductory Anthology* (Aldershot, Eng.: Scolar Press, 1989), p. 13.

21 Maser, "Introduction," in Ripa, *Iconologia*, pp. ix, vii.

22 Dacos, *Loggia of Raphael*, p. 106.

23 Ibid., p. 29.

24 Gombrich, *Symbolic Images*, p. 20.

25 Alain Gruber, *The History of Decorative Arts: The Renaissance and Mannerism in Europe* (New York: Abbeville Press, 1994), pp. 218–19.

26 Sheard, *Antiquity in the Renaissance*, n.p.

27 Pierre Grimal, *The Dictionary of Classical Mythology*, trans. A. R. Maxwell-Hyslop (Oxford and New York: Blackwell, 1986), 272.

28 Ripa, *Iconologia*, no. 79, "Peace."

29 Ibid., no. 26, "Patriotism"; no. 56, "Magnificence."

30 Ibid., no. 64, "Magnanimity."

31 Ibid., no. 169, "Revenge."

32 Alciati, *A Book of Emblems*, p. 32.

33 James Hall, *Dictionary of Subjects and Symbols in Art* (New York: Harper and Row, 1974, paperback edition), p. 110.

34 Ibid., p. 209.

35 Ibid.

36 Ripa, *Iconologia*, no. 36, "Perspicacity."

37 Wind, *Pagan Mysteries*, p. 122.

38 Hall, *Dictionary of Subjects and Symbols*, p. 217.

39 Grimal, *Dictionary of Classical Mythology*, p. 464–65.

40 Gombrich, *Symbolic Images*, p. 108.

41 Hall, *Dictionary of Subjects and Symbols*, pp. 238, 280.

42 Ibid., pp. 109, 294.

43 Ibid., p. 319.

44 Grimal, *Dictionary of Classical Mythology*, p. 153.

45 Hall, *Dictionary of Subjects and Symbols*, p. 227.

46 Alciati, *A Book of Emblems*, p. 137.

47 Ibid., p. 91.

48 Ripa, *Iconologia*, no. 132, "Debauchery."

49 Wind, *Pagan Mysteries*, pp. 145–46.

50 Hall, *Dictionary of Subjects and Symbols*, p. 127.

51 Ibid., p. 254.

52 Ripa, *Iconologia*, no. 120, "Justice."

53 Ibid., no. 175, "Hope."

54 Hall, *Dictionary of Subjects and Symbols*, p. 284.

55 Ibid., p. 280.

56 See Maurice Scève, *Delie, obiect de plvs havlte vertv* (Lyons, 1544); no. 13, in Moseley, *A Century of Emblems*, p. 66.

57 Ripa, *Iconologia*, no. 50, "Truth"; no. 140, "Reward."

58 Hall, *Dictionary of Subjects and Symbols*, p. 17.

59 Ripa, *Iconologia*, no. 52, "Friendship."

60 Hall, *Dictionary of Subjects and Symbols*, p. 249.

61 Ibid., p. 62.

62 Ripa, *Iconologia*, no. 28, "Joy"; no. 34, "Abundance."

Charissa Bremer-David

Tapestries at the Flint Institute of Arts:
The Story of Rinaldo and Armida

The narrative of the tapestry cycle known as *The Story of Rinaldo and Armida* derives from a longer text titled *Gerusalemme Liberata* (*Jerusalem Delivered*) originally written in the Tuscan dialect by Torquato Tasso in 1581.[1] The literary work was an epic poem that commemorated, and mythologized, the First Crusade (1095–99) when Christian knights, led by Godfrey de Bouillon (ca. 1058–1100), recaptured Jerusalem from Saracen control. Loosely based on historical fact, it was a fictionalized account composed in the chivalric tradition that grappled with the conflicting demands of duty versus desire. Inspired, to a degree, by the classical epics of Homer and Virgil, *Jerusalem Delivered* promoted the martial values of valor and action above rest and repose, of doing one's duty for the greater good despite the personal costs, and of fighting for one's honor before following one's heart— timeless themes that Tasso updated with the Christian belief in the divine might of the true god against malevolence and dark magic.

The ten-piece tapestry cycle (cats. 1–10) corresponds to just the last six of the poem's twenty long cantos or chapters, although Tasso introduced its main characters earlier in the narrative. Armida, the Saracen princess of Damascus, is a formidable opponent of the crusaders; head of a large force of Syrian soldiers, she is also a beguiling beauty who uses her feminine charms to manipulate and exploit the innate chivalry of the Christian knights to her advantage. Moreover, she is a powerful enchantress and sorceress who can control the weather, cast spells to ensnare the unsuspecting (see fig. 1), create and sustain sophisticated visual illusions, fly through the air on a magical chariot, and call upon dark powers in her fight against her enemies. Vengeful and impulsive, she embodies the characteristic then ascribed to pagans of being driven by raw emotion and uncontrolled desire.[2] But the well-intentioned Christian knight Rinaldo is also headstrong and impetuous. After killing his fellow crusader Gernando in a duel, he exiles himself from the camp of Godfrey de Bouillon. In the course of his wanderings, he comes upon a troop of Armida's soldiers escorting a band of captured crusaders. Despite the unfavorable odds, Rinaldo attacks and kills the Saracens and releases the prisoners. While this brave act restores Godfrey de Bouillon's esteem for Rinaldo, it provokes the wrath of Armida.

Fig. 1. Simon Vouet (1590–1649), designer; woven at the Faubourg Saint-Germain tapestry workshop (active 1633–67/68), detail of "Rinaldo Carried to Armida's Enchanted Chariot," from the *The Story of Rinaldo and Armida* tapestry cycle, 1633–37 (cat. 2)

The compositions of the tapestries take up Tasso's story, which, at this point, depart from any semblance of historical fact. The ensuing tale becomes an edifying subtext as the two enemies, Rinaldo and Armida, first succumb to, and then overcome, their carnal passions. Through the characters' experiences of complex physical struggles and emotional conflicts, creatively told as a shorter story involving fantastic creatures and supernatural forces within the greater narrative, Tasso explored a range of human feelings that resonated with his contemporary audience. He was deeply concerned with developing the moral strengths of his fictional protagonists who, in facing numerous personal trials and challenges, become models of virtuous behavior for his readers. Ultimately, in the tradition of Horace, Tasso meant to instruct as well as delight.[3]

Visual Sources and the Design of the Tapestries

Cartoons for a series of tapestries portraying *The Story of Rinaldo and Armida* were designed by French artist Simon Vouet (1590–1649) after his slightly earlier cycle of decorative panels of the same subject, which he painted in 1631 for the *galerie* of the château de Chessy. The panels of the earlier cycle, which still survive (though in a different location; see figs. 2, 3), were considerably smaller in size than the cartoons, since they were intended as insets into the wooden paneling of the *galerie*, where they were complemented by narrow sectional frames decorated with painted landscapes, floral garlands, and ornamental motifs.[4]

The château de Chessy was the country residence of Henry de Fourcy (d. 1638?), an important civil and court official in the circle of King Louis XIII (1601–1643, r. from 1610); he served as president of inquests at the Parlement of Paris and as the superintendent of the king's building works from 1625 (*président aux Enquêtes au Parlement de Paris* and

surintendant des Bâtiments du Roi). In this latter role, de Fourcy was intimately involved with the architectural and artistic patronage of the Crown, and he would have been aware of the king's recall of Vouet from Italy to France in 1627.[5] Furthermore, he would have been the central administrator for the Crown's commissions of tapestry designs from this artist upon his return to Paris. Vouet was prolifically productive in these years, supplying designs for at least five, or possibly seven, different series of diverse subjects.[6] De Fourcy, because of his official capacity and influence, was in a position of power and could have personally commanded a private commission of *Rinaldo and Armida* panels from Vouet.[7]

The selection of Tasso's epic poem as a narrative for the medium of tapestry was driven by the wide popularity that the literary work still enjoyed in the first half of the seventeenth century. Having been translated into both French and English by 1600, it served as the inspiration for many artistic projects, including a musical ballet by René Bordier (d. 1658) that was dedicated in 1617 to Louis XIII, and several paintings by a contemporary of Vouet's working in Rome, Nicolas Poussin (1594–1665).[8] Its prolonged popularity was demonstrated by yet another French translation in 1626, the *Hiérusalem deslivrée*, by Jean Baudoin (?1590–1650).[9] Vouet had undoubtedly also read recent Italian editions while he was in Italy from 1614 to 1627, a supposition that is likely, judging from the similarity between some aspects of Vouet's compositions and the engraved illustrations that accompanied the Italian editions. There are several close pictorial correspondences, for instance, between Vouet's "Rinaldo and His Companions Leave the Enchanted Isle" (fig. 4 and cat. 7) and the etching of the same scene, dating to about 1623–25, by Antonio Tempesta (1555–1630; fig. 5).[10] It was exactly this sort of knowledge and familiarity with

Italian sources, literary and visual, that increased Vouet's reputation in Parisian artistic circles.[11]

Moreover, Vouet brought a personal knowledge of classical antiquity to the project, which was expressed in certain details of the architectural and sculptural features in the settings of some scenes. In "Carlo and Ubaldo at the Fountain of Laughter" (cat. 4), for example, there is a carved stone caryatid of an armless satyr at the far side of the fountain wall (fig. 6). This figure ultimately derives from two antique life-size Pans, sculpted as supporting figures known as telamon, that were excavated just outside Rome before 1481 and that were known in humanist and artistic circles since their installation in 1518 in the courtyard of the Palazzo della Valle di Cantone in Rome, belonging to Cardinal Andrea della Valle (1463–1534, cardinal from 1517).[12] These armless satyrs were recorded in this location by Maerten van Heemskerck (1498–1574) in a drawing dating from the 1530s (fig. 7).[13]

Some small-scale preparatory sketches by Vouet for *The Story of Rinaldo and Armida* survive in the Musée du Louvre, notably a study for the head of the sleeping Rinaldo (fig. 8) in "Rinaldo Carried to Armida's Enchanted Chariot" (cat. 2); the standing nymph (fig. 9) in "Carlo and Ubaldo at the Fountain of Laughter" (cat. 4); the head of Armida in "Carlo and Ubaldo Spy on the Lovers" (cat. 5); one sketch formerly attributed to Vouet relating to one of the wrestling satyrs in the lower-right corner of each border (fig. 10).[14] Apparently, the full-size painted cartoons for the tapestries no longer survive, but they were executed in his studio between 1631 and 1635, as indicated by documentary evidence listing cartoons in the 1635 after-death inventory of Charles de Comans (d. 1634), director of the Faubourg Saint-Marcel weaving atelier, and because weavings of the subjects were on the looms by 1635 for the king's commission in another Parisian tapestry atelier, that of Girard Laurent the Younger (ca. 1588–1670) and Maurice Dubout the Younger (active until 1657), located in the Louvre galleries.[15] Due to the immense scale of the overall compositional concept for the entire series, whose combined linear length totaled more than 107 feet, assistants

From left to right:

Fig. 8. Simon Vouet, Two studies of the head of Rinaldo tilted back toward the left, early 1630s; black chalk with white chalk highlights, 14.1 x 14.2 cm. Musée du Louvre, Paris (RF28144). Photo © Réunion des Musées Nationaux / Art Resource, NY. Photo: Jean-Gilles Berizzi

Fig. 9. Simon Vouet, Half-length drawing of nude nymph, early 1630s; black chalk with white chalk highlights, 25.4 x 16.7 cm. Musée du Louvre, Paris (RF14729, recto). Photo © Réunion des Musées Nationaux / Art Resource, NY. Photo: Madeleine Coursaget

Fig. 10. Formerly attributed to Simon Vouet, Head of reclining satyr, black chalk with white highlights, 22.8 x 25.7 cm. Musée du Louvre, Paris (RF14723, recto). Photo © Réunion des Musées Nationaux / Art Resource, NY. Photo: Madeleine Coursaget

in Vouet's workshop helped in preparing the cartoons. A contemporary chronicler, André Félibien (1619–1695), named two landscape painters who may have collaborated on the cartoons: François Bellin (or Belin, d. 1661, a pupil of the Antwerp painter Fouquières) and Pierre Patel (d. 1676), who often painted scenes of classical ruins.[16] In general, Vouet had many assistant painters in his workshop; one of those was Pierre Van Boucle (d. 1673), who may have painted the figures in the borders. Vouet would have closely supervised the weaving of the tapestries, as their color matches those of the painted models in many places.[17]

In terms of composition, the tapestries are dominated by dramatic, large-scale human figures in the foreground of the lush landscapes of a magical island and the Holy Land. Each scene is framed by tree trunks, rocky outcrops, caves, or theatrical swags of curtain, while the wide borders provide a unifying and rhythmic structure from one tapestry to the next. The psychological tension of the story is played out through the broad gestures of the figural forms, accentuated by the dramatic play of light and shadow. Vouet's *Story of Rinaldo and Armida* has been interpreted as pictorial poetry or the visual expression of a literary form, lyric poetry.[18]

When one compares Vouet's Baroque artistic vision to Tasso's Renaissance text, it becomes immediately apparent that Vouet's sensibilities prized the internal struggles of the protagonists above the overall military narrative about the control of Jerusalem. There are no battle scenes in the tapestry cycle, no tangles of combatants and war horses. Vouet's cycle—and the tapestries woven after it—does not portray the stratagems and challenges faced by the crusaders in their call to arms in Palestine. The images focus instead on the emotional pleasure and pain experienced in the hearts of two enemies who, despite mortal antagonisms, become lovers—the pagan princess and sorceress Armida and the Christian knight Rinaldo. Vouet expands upon the moral of Tasso's story by adding another layer of meaning: virtuous love and compassion ultimately triumph over worldly strife and death.

Fig. 11. Detail of cat. 4

Fig. 12. Detail of cat. 1

The Iconography of the Borders

Elements of *The Story of Rinaldo and Armida* are reinforced through the design of the broad borders, in grisaille and dark blue, which suggest an illusion of three-dimensional molded stucco frames (see fig. 11). These borders are conceived as a progression of motifs that seem to project from the picture plane in various degrees of gradation. The outer perimeter on all four sides (but only two in the *entrefenêtres*, which lack side borders) consists of concentric monochromatic "moldings" of a string of hearts (fig. 12), acanthus-leaf scrolls, foliated guilloche, and a string of beads, respectively (from the outermost section of the border). These lead the eye toward the inner field of dark blue, in which rinceaux and trailing ivy vines intertwine. In the main tapestries, each upper corner of the border contains a full figure of a winged female bearing trumpets, as allegories of Fame (figs. 13, 14), while each lower corner bears a pair of wrestling horned satyrs, which may represent the baser, bacchanalian carnal lusts. The midpoint of each length of border on the main tapestries (and of the top and bottom borders on the *entrefenêtres*) is punctuated by a cartouche adorned with putti bearing attributes (see figs. 15–17). A near-contemporary emblem book from the 1640s helps to identify these attributes and to decode their meaning.[19] The laurel wreath held by the winged putti in the top borders, as in fig. 15 (and the laurel garland they hold suspended below the cartouche in the bottom borders, as in fig. 17), refers to the ancient Roman god Apollo and symbolizes victory as well as the virtuous love that encompasses the cardinal virtues of Justice, Prudence, Fortitude, and Temperance. Their oak wreaths and oak garlands allude to the omnipotence of Jupiter and signify glorious love as well as valor in combat. Their palm branches illustrate a vexatious, worldly love, as between humans who, in a *combat d'amour*, annoy each other by fighting over a palm branch. Medieval tradition adds another layer of meaning, since a palm branch was also the symbol of religious pilgrimage, a suitable association for an epic concerning the First Crusade. The single putto above the cartouche in each side border holds thick branches of oak leaves and acorns, reiterating the themes of glorious love and valor in combat (see fig. 16). Centrally positioned in each lower border, a military trophy composed of a plumed helmet, banners, and battering rams symbolizes the military goals of the crusading knights in Tasso's epic poem (fig. 17).

The moralizing messages of *The Story of Rinaldo and Armida* are reinforced further through the presence of small-scale allegorical figures within the cartouches. A total of ten

Top, left to right: Figs. 13 and 14.
Details of cat. 2, showing Fame

Middle, left to right: Fig. 15.
Detail of cat. 4, putti and border
cartouche with Muse Urania

Fig. 16. Detail of cat. 4, putto and
border cartouche with Victoria

Lower left: Fig. 17. Detail of cat. 3,
putti and border cartouche with
Prudence

Clockwise, from left:
Fig. 18. Detail of cat. 6, Calliope in border cartouche

Fig. 19. Detail of cat. 4, Urania in top border cartouche

Fig. 20. Detail of cat. 4, Navigation or the Sciences in right side border cartouche

figures repeat throughout these cartouches in random order across the set of tapestries. They can be grouped broadly into four categories spanning both ancient classical and Christian personifications: classical gods, muses, cardinal virtues, and worldly achievements. Though seemingly disparate, their identities or characteristics do have relevance to the overall themes of *Jerusalem Delivered*. Three classical, ancient Roman gods are represented: Mercury, protector of travelers, with his winged feet and caduceus (inferring agility and fleetness); Minerva, goddess of wisdom, with her spear and shield emblazoned with the head of Medusa (virtue and military concord); and Mars, god of war, with the marshal's baton and military trophies (fortitude and valor). There are two muses: Calliope (fig. 18), with the writing tablet (epic poetry) and the striding Urania (fig. 19), with an armillary sphere and compass (astronomy).[20] Three of the cardinal virtues are portrayed: Fortitude, with a column; Justice, with the sword and balance scales; and Prudence, with the mirror and serpent (see fig. 17). The last category—worldly achievements—poses some challenges of identification. The personification of one worldly achievement is readily discernible: Victoria, with her wreath and palm (victory) (see fig. 16). The last figure, however, is puzzling: she appears to be a repetition of the muse Urania (though seated here, holding an armillary sphere but no compass), but since one tapestry, "Carlo and Ubaldo at the Fountain of Laughter" (cat. 4), bears both the striding and the seated variants within two of its cartouches (figs. 19, 20), it doesn't seem likely that both figures should represent Urania. Perhaps, this second figure personifies Navigation (which, at that time, was dependent upon the movement of the celestial bodies), a suitable theme for crusaders to the Holy Land and for the mariners Carlo and Ubaldo, or else the Sciences, particularly the quadrivium (the four liberal arts of astronomy, arithmetic, geometry, and music).

Production of *The Story of Rinaldo and Armida* Tapestries

Simon Vouet's designs for *The Story of Rinaldo and Armida* proved highly successful in the medium of tapestry, as is evident from the fact that twenty-one surviving sets and fourteen different border types have been identified.[21] The series was woven until about 1660 in at least four different workshops, three of them in Paris and one in Amiens: in the Louvre galleries under the direction of Maurice Dubout the Younger and Girard Laurent the Younger; in the Faubourg Saint-Germain workshop under the direction of Raphaël de La Planche (see fig. 21); in the Faubourg Saint-Marcel workshop operating under Charles

de Comans (d. 1634), then under Alexandre de Comans (active 1635–50) and his brother Hippolyte; and in the Comans's subsidiary workshop located in the town of Amiens. Certain border types can be traced or localized to the production of these distinct workshops.[22] The French royal inventory compiled between 1663 and 1666 records that, by then, the Crown possessed three sets of these tapestries: one consisting of eight hangings woven with silver-gilt metallic thread produced on the Dubout and Laurent looms in the Louvre galleries; another consisting of six hangings, also woven with silver-gilt metallic thread, and with satyrs in the lower borders, produced under Raphaël de La Planche in the Faubourg Saint-Germain workshop; and a third set consisting of seven hangings woven without metallic thread.[23] None of these are preserved at present in the Mobilier National, the successor to the former royal Garde-Meuble de la Couronne (the king's household furnishing agency).

Of the surviving sets, the partial set of four preserved since 1874 in the château du Haras-du-Pin (Orne, Normandy) is interesting because details in its borders reveal the identities of its first owner and of the master weaver involved in its creation. The central cartouche in each lower border prominently displays the monogram of the patron who commissioned the set, the nobleman Jean II de Choisy (1571–1652, a councilor of state and the *receveur des finances de la Généralité de Caen*). Moreover, one of the hangings bears, in the outer blue *galon* (selvage edge), the initials of the weaver Jean Tayer (also known as Hans Taye, active in the Comans workshop at Faubourg Saint-Marcel).[24]

Documentary evidence indicates that, regardless of the workshop of origin, tapestry sets of *The Story of Rinaldo and Armida* normally consisted of eight or fewer hangings each; therefore, the set preserved in the Flint Institute of Arts is of exceptional significance. It is the only known set of this series comprising ten pieces, and it is also unique in having remained together, with its borders and selvage edges intact, for its entire history—from the moment it left the looms in the Faubourg Saint-Germain workshop in 1637 (see provenance on p. 84). Its commission represented a large and prestigious order for this new workshop, recently established in 1633 by Raphaël de La Planche when he separated from the operation in Faubourg Saint-Marcel that had been co-founded by two Flemings—his own father, François de La Planche (1573–1627), and his uncle, Marc de Comans (1563–1644)—in 1601 under the protection of King Henri IV (1553–1610, r. from 1589). In 1634, the Saint-Germain workshop already employed more than 120 workers; and many of these must have been highly skilled, experienced weavers, as the commission was completed in only four years.[25] Its overall measurement, of more than 178 square yards, indicates that the rate of weaving proceeded at a pace of about 44½ square yards per year. The number of looms dedicated to this commission is not known; but hypothetically, if there were ten looms, each 16 feet in length (so that three or four weavers could sit side-by-side and work simultaneously on one hanging), then each weaver would have produced about 1 to 1½ square yards per year.[26] The identities of these talented craftsmen remain unknown, as they left no individual weaver's marks.

It was a laborious process to interpret Vouet's painted cartoons in the medium of tapestry. The craftsmen were faced with an especially difficult challenge because, for hangings of this size, the technique required that each composition be woven from the back and sideways. Once the loom was set up with the undyed warps wrapped parallel along the two beams of its frame (like lyre strings spanning the extent of the textile's greater length, about 15 feet in this case), weavers interlaced colored wool and silk weft threads over and under them. As the colored threads gradually covered the warps, the narrative field evolved so that at first elements of a side border, then margins of sky and landscape, and finally human figures emerged visually, in an orientation perpendicular to that of the picture plane. Due to the loom structure, weavers faced the back side of the tapestry while working on it. When each tapestry was finished and displayed, suspended against a wall, the warp threads stretched horizontally from side to side, while the colored wool and silk wefts (which create the pictorial illusion) stretched vertically.

My thanks to the Flint Institute of Arts, especially John Henry, Director of the FIA, for the opportunity to contribute to this volume commemorating the fiftieth anniversary of the donation of the art collection and gallery from Viola E. Bray. Generous research support was provided by Tracee Glab, Associate Curator, and by Monique M. Desormeau, Curator of Education. Farther afield, Arnauld Brejon de Lavergnée, Directeur des collections at the Mobilier National, Paris, graciously confirmed several essential points.

1   The English translation of *Jerusalem Delivered* cited in this entry is by Edward Fairfax (1560–1635), published in London in 1600; the relevant verses from Fairfax's translation are provided in cats. 1–10 of the present volume. The book is available online as an eBook, courtesy of Project Gutenberg: www.gutenberg.org/dirs/3/9/392/392.txt, posted August 4, 2008. For a more recent English translation, see Torquato Tasso, *Jerusalem Delivered, Gerusalemme liberata*, ed. and trans. Anthony M. Esolen (Baltimore: The Johns Hopkins University Press, 2000).

2   Jonathan Unglaub, *Poussin and the Poetics of Painting: Pictorial Narrative and the Legacy of Tasso* (Cambridge and New York: Cambridge University Press, 2006), p. 205.

3   Rensselaer W. Lee, "Instruction and Delight," in Lee, *Ut Pictura Poesis: The Humanistic Theory of Painting* (New York: W. W. Norton & Company, Inc., 1967), pp. 32–34.

4   After the destruction of the château de Chessy (Seine-et-Marne), these smaller painted panels were transferred in the mid-1800s to the Guyot de Villeneuve residence, in the Place de Messine, Paris, where they were incorporated into the wooden wall paneling. Presently, they are in a private collection, Paris. See William R. Crelly, *The Painting of Simon Vouet* (New Haven and London: Yale University Press, 1962), pp. 104–6, 171, 205, illustrating the Vouet models as figures 125–130; and see also Jacques Thuillier et al., *Vouet*, exh. cat. (Paris: Galeries Nationales du Grand Palais, 1990), pp. 116–18, 489–525.

5   Jean Coural, *Chefs-d'œuvre de la Tapisserie Parisienne 1597–1662*, exh. cat. (Versailles: Orangerie de Versailles, 1967), p. 22.

6   Vouet produced designs for at least five, or possibly seven, tapestry series between 1627 and about 1643. The five known series are: *The Story of Rinaldo and Armida* in eight principal scenes after the cycle made for Henry de Fourcy in the Château de Chessy; *The Story of Ulysses* in a cycle of eight scenes made for the Paris hôtel of the superintendent of finance Claude de Bullion; *The Story of Theagenes and Chariclea* in twelve scenes after the cycle also made for Claude de Bullion; *The Loves of the Gods* in ten principal scenes, perhaps after the cycle made for the marshal Antoine Coeffier–Ruzé d'Effiat at the Château de Chilly; and *Stories from the Old Testament* in six scenes, commissioned by Louis XIII before 1643. Vouet is also associated with two more series, *The Story of Psyche* and *The Story of Adonis*, although little is known about their creation. See Isabelle Denis, "The Parisian Workshops, 1590–1650" and Jean Vittet, "Moses Rescued from the Nile" in *Tapestry in the Baroque: Threads of Splendor*, exh. cat., ed. Thomas P. Campbell (New York: Metropolitan Museum of Art, 2007), pp. 129–130, 163–169, and notes 42–43 on p. 139. See also Isabelle Denis, "Tenture de l'Ancien Testament," "Les Travaux d'Ulysse," and "Les Amours des Dieux" in *Lisses et délices: Chefs-d'oeuvre de la tapisserie de Henri IV à Louis XIV*, exh. cat. (Paris: Caisse nationale des monuments historiques et des sites,

1996), pp. 143–89; and Guy Delmarcel et al., *The Toms Collection: Tapestries of the Sixteenth to Nineteenth Centuries*, ed. Giselle Eberhard Cotton, trans. Irena Podleska and Geoffrey Peek (Lausanne. Switz.: Fondation Toms Pauli and Zurich, Switz.: Niggli, 2010), p. 161 and notes 20–21 on p. 165.

7   Initially, Henry de Fourcy commissioned a different artist, Quentin Varin (ca. 1570–1634), to paint a *Story of Rinaldo and Armida*, and it is not known exactly why or how the project was transferred to Simon Vouet. For one theory, see Pascal-François Bertrand, *Les tapisseries des Barberini et la decoration d'intérieur dans la Rome baroque* (Turnhout, Belgium: Brepols, 2005), p. 119 and note 216 on p. 181.

8   According to Lavalle, the poem was translated into French as early as 1600 by Jacques Corbin, as *La suite et la fin des amours d'Armide et d'Herminie*. This was followed by an anonymous translation in 1620 titled *Le Renauld fortuné, histoire consécutive de la Hierusalem délivrée du signeur T. Tasso*. See Denis Lavalle, "Simon Vouet et le tapisserie," in *Vouet*, exh. cat., ed. Jacques Thuillier (Paris: Galeries Nationales du Grand Palais, 1990), pp. 512–13. Edward Fairfax's first English translation dates to 1594 (see note 1). Concerning Poussin's portrayal of scenes from *The Story of Rinaldo and Armida*, see Unglaub, *Poussin and the Poetics of Painting*, pp. 3, 62–70, and note 10 on p. 228, note 55 on p. 236, and illustrated fig. 21 on p. 67.

9   Coincidentally, Jean Baudoin, the French translator of the 1626 edition of the poem was also the translator of Cesar

Ripa's book of emblems, *Iconologie ou Explication Nouvelle de Plusieurs Images, Emblems, et autres Figures ... Tirée des Recherches & des Figures de Cesar Ripa*, which codified so many of the allegorical figures incorporated into the border designs of this series.

10 Unglaub, *Poussin and the Poetics of Painting*, p. 66 and figs. 19 and 20.

11 For more on Vouet's familiarity with antique, Renaissance, and Baroque sources, see Lee, "Rinaldo and Armida," in *Ut pictura poesis*, pp. 48–56.

12 The figures were brought by the Medici in 1584 to Florence and are now, with reconstructed arms, in the Capitoline Museum, Rome. See Francis Haskell and Nicholas Penny, *Taste and the Antique: The Lure of Classical Sculpture, 1500–1900* (New Haven and London: Yale University Press, 1981), p. 12, fig. 6, and pp. 301–3, no. 75. See also Kathleen Wren Christian, "Instauratio and Pietas: The della Valle Collections of Ancient Sculpture," in Nicholas Penny and Eike D. Schmidt, eds., *Collecting Sculpture in Early Modern Europe* (Washington, D.C.: National Gallery of Art, 2008), pp. 33–65.

13 Now in the Kupferstichkabinett, Bildarchiv, Preußischer Kulturbesitz, Berlin, inv. no. 79.D.2, fol. 20r.

14 All in the Musée du Louvre, Département des Arts graphiques, inv. nos., respectively, RF 28144 recto, RF 14729 recto, RF 28215 recto, RF 28137 recto, and RF 14723 recto. Images are viewable at the online collection database of the Musée du Louvre: http://arts-graphiques.louvre.fr. See also Barbara Brejon de Lavergnée, *Dessins de Simon Vouet, 1590–1649* (Paris: Réunion des Musées Nationaux, 1987), especially pp. 54–59, 85, and 209. The author did not include the drawing of the wrestling satyr (inv. no. RF14723) in this volume.

15 Coural, *Chefs-d'œuvre de la Tapisserie Parisienne 1597–1662*, pp. 18, 20. Two types of cartoons appear in these documents: nine unspecified scenes with small figures and three other scenes with large figures. However, the figures in the narrative fields of all the extant tapestries are large-scale.

16 Lavalle, "Simon Vouet et le tapisserie," p. 492; Bertrand, *Les tapisseries des Barberini et la decoration d'intérieur dans la Rome baroque*, pp. 163–69; Delmarcel et al., *The Toms Collection*, cat. no. 54, pp. 160–65.

17 Lavalle, "Simon Vouet et le tapisserie," p. 498.

18 In reference to Horace's simile in the *Ars poetica*, "ut pictura poesis" (or "as is painting so is poetry"), see Lee, *Ut pictura poesis*, p. 3.

19 J[ean] Baudoin (translator), *Iconologie, ou Explication Nouvelle de Plusieurs Images, Emblems, et autres Figures ... Tirée des Recherches & des Figures de Cesar Ripa* (Paris: Mathieu Guillemot, 1644; reprint edition, Dijon: Faton, 1999), pp. 98–99, 102, 104.

20 It is significant that the artist who designed the cycle, Simon Vouet, painted the same two muses, Urania (without a compass) and Calliope, together with putti holding laurel wreaths, in an allegory of the arts and sciences in 1634. The painting is now in the National Gallery, Washington, D.C., Samuel H. Kress Collection, 1961.9.61.

21 For a summary of the extant hangings, see Delmarcel et al., *The Toms Collection*, cat. no. 54, pp. 160–65; and Bertrand, *Les tapisseries des Barberini et la decoration d'intérieur dans la Rome baroque*, notes 233–35 and 237 on pp. 182–83.

22 For weavings that share the same type of border as that on the set in the Flint Institute of Arts, see Delmarcel et al., *The Toms Collection*, note 31 on p. 165.

23 Jules Guiffrey, *Inventaire général du Mobilier de la Couronne sous Louis XIV (1663–1715)*, vol. 1 (Paris: Société d'Encouragement pour la propagation des livre d'art, 1885), no. 13 on p. 295, no. 21 on p. 297, and no. 1 on p. 332; Maurice Fenaille et al., *État général des tapisseries de la Manufacture des Gobelins depuis son origine jusqu'à nos jours, 1600–1900* (Paris: Imprimerie nationale, 1923), vol. 1, pp. 322–24; and Jean Vittet and Arnauld Brejon de Lavergnée, *La collection de tapisseries de Louis XIV* (Dijon: Faton, 2010), pp. 40–41, 58–59, 295.

24 See Lavalle, "Simon Vouet et le tapisserie," pp. 512–18. On Jean Tayer, see Denis, "Diana and Apollo Slaying the Children of Niobe," p. 150. Recent scholarship has pointed out that the design of this border appears on other tapestry series portraying different subjects woven in Paris before the arrival of Vouet in 1627, and therefore it is not of Vouet's invention. See Delmarcel et al., *The Toms Collection*, cat. no. 54 on p. 164, and notes 26 and 34 on p. 165. Another set of four *Story of Rinaldo and Armida* tapestries survives intact in the château de Châteaudun (Eure-et-Loire), woven in the Saint-Marcel workshop under the direction of Alexandre de Comans, with borders containing floral garlands. For an illustration of its wide version of "Rinaldo Carried to Armida's Enchanted Chariot," see Denis, "The Parisian Workshops, 1590–1650," fig. 65 on p. 129.

25 On the Faubourg Saint-Germain workshop, see Denis, "The Parisian Workshops, 1590–1650," p. 128.

26 Regarding the rate of productivity at this time, Delmarcel calculated that one Flemish weaver could produce a tapestry measuring 11' 3" x 16' 5" (345 x 500 cm) in twenty-one months if the design was of average complexity and the gauge of the wool was of medium thickness, and, therefore, if three weavers worked on the piece together, it could be finished in seven months; Guy Delmarcel, *Flemish Tapestry* (New York: Harry N. Abrams, 1999), p. 14. However, Campbell noted that this estimate did not include the time required to prepare the loom; Thomas P. Campbell, *Tapestry in the Renaissance: Art and Magnificence* (New York: Metropolitan Museum of Art, 2002), p. 6.

Arnauld Brejon de Lavergnée

The Position of Simon Vouet in French Tapestry

Simon Vouet's position in French and European tapestry has been undergoing a reevaluation for some forty years (since a major exhibition of French tapestries in 1967, to be exact).[1] Until a definitive collection of Vouet's works is established, this reevaluation will remain incomplete. The exhibition in 1996 at the château de Chambord (Loir-et-Cher, France), for example, presented proof of a "new" tapestry that he designed, *The Loves of the Gods*,[2] which was never published in early twentieth-century catalogues of French tapestry. Although Vouet (1590–1649) was the *premier peintre du roi* (first painter to the king), his design work for tapestries has sometimes been overlooked compared to the attention given designs made for the king by Flemish painter Peter Paul Rubens (1577–1640). Vouet, called back from his ten-year stay in Italy in 1627 by King Louis XIII (1601–1643, r. from 1610), provided designs for five, or possibly seven, tapestry series between 1627 and about 1643. The designs include the following: *The Story of Rinaldo and Armida* (see fig. 1); *The Story of Ulysses*; *The Story of Theagenes and Chariclea*; *The Loves of the Gods*; and *Stories from the Old Testament*.

Jacques Thuillier, in his introduction to the catalogue of the exhibition in 1967, presented a balanced assessment of the relationship of tapestry to painting in these words: "We are truly a long way from a 'minor' art: the same painters worked simultaneously in tapestry and painting, with the same intentions and the same approach. And it sometimes happened that tapestry took precedence: in the *Stories from the Old Testament* that Vouet designed only for weavers, he may have gotten carried away by the complex challenge of his very beautiful settings as if the painter had found in tapestry the medium in which he could show his full mastery, even more than in the often limited space available over a mantelpiece for a painting."[3]

In a review of that exhibition, Bertrand Jestaz insisted on Vouet's originality in this field:

It is from another painter, Simon Vouet, that a new style was to be born, and the exhibition at Versailles so clearly recognizes his superiority that it will henceforth be necessary to consider 1627, the date of his return to France, as the most important date in the history of tapestry production in Paris. If one can theorize in broad terms about works in which art is expressed by small details, I would emphasize three innovations that seem crucial:

- The predominance of landscape (particularly forest landscapes) over human figures (the number of figures is usually reduced);

Fig. 1. Simon Vouet (1590–1649), designer; woven at the Faubourg Saint-Germain tapestry workshop (active 1633–67/68), detail of "Rinaldo Views His Image in the Diamond Shield," from the *The Story of Rinaldo and Armida* tapestry cycle, 1633–37 (cat. 6)

- The use of light, which is no longer an indirect light intended to shape figures in an artificial way but rather a kind of breath that penetrates the whole composition and orients it in a definite direction … ;
- The placing in the foreground of one dark object—usually a tree—which rises the whole height of the scene, in view of which the subject in bright light can move into the middle distance and stand out against a dark background or one in half-tones and still allow the possibilities of bright details in the background.

Thus Vouet's figures *glimmer* in an undergrowth alive with shadows and bright flashes in which the light gets deeper as much as it slips in from the sides. To understand the full importance and merit of Vouet's approach, it is sufficient to compare his impression of constant movement based on contrast and an absence of shaded tones with the weak play of light and dark which, previous to him, had controlled the relationship between figures and the background.[4]

Denis Lavalle presented some magnificent tapestries by Vouet in an exhibition of his works that was held in the Grand Palais, Paris, in 1990–91.[5] The set of four tapestries from the cycle of *The Story of Rinaldo and Armida* (château du Haras-du-Pin, Orne, Normandy), in particular, impressed visitors to the exhibition. Lavalle pointed out how Vouet took into account scale, viewing position, and materials available when he created his designs:

The tapestry presented the scale necessary for a good reading; it also offered the possibility of keeping in view the entirety of a cycle, of showing the definite relations between different episodes. Of course, to interpret painted interiors [in the medium of tapestry] was not an easy job. It was necessary not only to take into account the work of the weavers but also the nature of the actual materials. The numerous cartoons and sketches found in Vouet's records show a distinctive awareness of these problems, all the more so since he did not seek to start making mere copies of his works, but rather wanted to make their poetry come alive by relying on the correct language of tapestry while seeking a happy meeting between his stylistic forms and the effects inherent in the weaving of wool and silk. He did not hesitate to work as well with the type of ornamentation developed by the tapestry industry and took into account the established models for borders.[6]

Since then, research has begun in other areas—the tapestries' historical background, the commissions, and the origin of their creation. Pascal-François Bertrand, in his important 2005 work on the Barberini tapestries, analyzed *The Story of Rinaldo and Armida* tapestry cycle (now in the Flint Institute of Arts).[7] The new digital photography of the FIA tapestries in this book provides striking evidence for his views (see cats. 1–10). Bertrand presented his analysis of Vouet's tapestries in a wide-ranging historical context that included Cardinal Francesco Barberini (1597–1679, cardinal from 1623) and his interest in tapestry; the tapestries used in the decoration of the residences of Pope Urban VIII's nephews; and the great series of tapestries belonging to the Barberini family and their models or cartoons. His conclusion is not surprising: that tapestry designed by Vouet holds its own in comparison with those by Rubens or by Italian painter Pietro da Cortona (1596–1669). In the seventeenth century, Vouet was not the only painter designing tapestries for the king. Earlier, in 1622, while Rubens was in Paris to execute a cycle of paintings for Marie de' Medici (1575–1624; mother and regent of Louis XIII in 1610), he was commissioned to design twelve scenes for tapestries on the theme of the Roman Emperor Constantine. Seven of these tapestries (now in the Philadelphia Museum of Art) were presented by Louis XIII in 1625 to Cardinal Barberini. In 1630, Barberini commissioned Pietro to design six panels to complete the set (also now in Philadelphia).

Another example of a first-rate understanding of the origins of these works is Jean Vittet's study of *Moses Rescued from the Nile* (Musée du Louvre, Paris) in the catalogue for a 2007 exhibition at the Metropolitan Museum of Art.[8] Many seventeenth-century patrons and collectors, among them Jacques-Auguste de Thou and Jean de Choisy, wanted to own a copy of this tapestry based on an episode from the Old Testament, which had been commissioned by Louis XIII and intended from the beginning for the galleries of the Louvre. The execution of this work, however, was later than originally thought and should not be dated to the years immediately following Vouet's return to France.

The 2010 catalogue of the tapestries from the collection of Louis XIV (1638–1715, r. from 1643)[9] includes several discoveries about Vouet, including a reference to a tapestry that is no longer extant from a set of six tapestries to be hung above doors, three of them showing the arms of France and Navarre accompanied by Mars and Minerva and the other three showing a palm frond heaped with war trophies and accompanied by two figures of Fame holding a crown. This tapestry corresponds to an entry in the inventory of the estate of Anne Pielegrain (d. 1635), wife of Girard Laurent, master weaver with a workshop in the galleries of the Louvre. Five landscape tapestries richly decorated with greenery, based on a "design by Vouet," have been shown to be related to several tapestries that have recently come up for sale. At the same time, the right-hand section of a tapestry based

on Vouet's *The Greeks at Circe's Table* (in the Court of Appeals in Riom, in the Auvergne), was connected by an artificially attached landscape to the left-hand section, which is full of figures.[10] From time to time other tapestries have resurfaced (such as those of Gallery Kraemer in Paris), some with monograms that appear on the borders that still need to be identified (for example, the monogram "BCM" on *The Sacrifice of Abraham*, in the château of Châteaudun, France).

My last and most important point is about the origin of the weavings. Unfortunately the cartoons, painted on a scale of 1:1, disappeared a long time ago. We do not yet know whether the artisans were professional painters of cartoons, skilled manual workers, or even several of the painters mentioned by André Félibien (court historian to Louis XIV) such as Jean Cotelle, François Vandrisse, Pierre Patel, and François Belin. A fair number of the remaining preliminary sketches of various figures have been studied by Barbara Brejon de Lavergnée.[11] For the tapestry cycle of *Stories from the Old Testament*, there still exist no less than nineteen sketches; for that of *The Story of Rinaldo and Armida*, ten; for the *Story of Ulysses*, no more than five each (see fig. 2), and for the *Story of Theagenes and Chariclea*, five. Those that have disappeared are important, but even without them one can truly say that the preliminary work was carefully done: we can be certain that Vouet controlled very closely the work of the artisans and the weavers, and he would have left nothing to chance in the complete development of his designs. He not only planned his paintings but the tapestries and the painted interiors as well. For the tapestry cycle of *The Story of Rinaldo and Armida* in the FIA, one has the great fortune to have the paintings on which the tapestries were based, which were originally installed in the gallery of the château de Chessy (Seine-et-Marne) and later elegantly rehung in a private home in Paris at the beginning of the twentieth century (see fig. 3).[12]

This latest publication on the tapestries in the Flint Institute of Arts will certainly help us to reevaluate Vouet's position in the art of European tapestry of the classical age. In the Paris of the 1630s, the tapestry cycle of *Rinaldo and Armida* seemed extremely innovative compared with royal commissions that had been woven previously, such as *Artemisia* or *Coriolanus* by French painter Henri Lerambert (ca. 1550–1609) or the rather austere *Constantine* tapestry cycle based on Rubens's designs. The king and his contemporaries were

not mistaken in their appreciation for Vouet's work: the inventory of Louis XIV's collection lists three sets of tapestries of *The Story of Rinaldo and Armida*[13] (two sets of which were woven with silver-gilt thread); and a number of private individuals also bought sets from the workshop in the Faubourg Saint-Marcel.[14] In other words, *Rinaldo and Armida* has surpassed *Artemisia*, *Coriolanus*, and *Constantine* in terms of innovation and popularity.

This essay was translated from the French by R. J. Kelly, III.

1 Jacques Thuillier, "Introduction," in Jean Coural, *Chefs-d'oeuvre de la Tapisserie Parisienne, 1597–1662*, exh. cat. (Versailles: Orangerie de Versailles, 1967).

2 *Lisses et délices: Chefs-d'oeuvre de la tapisserie de Henri IV á Louis XIV* (Paris: Caisse Nationale des monuments historiques et des sites, 1996), pp. 169–89. Two earlier catalogues that did not include Vouet's *The Loves of the Gods* are Fenaille 1923 and Heinrich Gobel, *Wandteppiche* (Leipzig: Klinkhardt & Biermann, 1923–).

3 Thuillier, "Introduction," in Coural, *Chefs-d'oeuvre*, p. 11.

4 Bertrand Jestaz, "La Tapisserie française, 1597–1662," *Revue de l'Art*, no. 1/2 (Paris: Flammarion, 1968): 133.

5 Denis Lavalle, "Tapisseries," in *Vouet*, exh. cat. (Paris: Galeries nationales du Grand Palais, 1990), nos. 142–52.

6 Ibid., p. 498. The *Rinaldo and Armida* cycle was on loan from the château du Haras-du-Pin (Orne, Normandy).

7 Pascal-François Bertrand, *Les tapisseries des Barberini et la decoration d'intérieur dans la Rome baroque* (Turnhout: Brepols, 2005).

8 Jean Vittet, entry no. 15: "Moses Rescued from the Nile," in *Tapestry in the Baroque: Threads of Splendor*, exh. cat. (New York: Metropolitan Museum of Art, 2007), p. 163.

9 Jean Vittet and Arnauld Brejon de Lavergnée, with Monique de Savignac, *La collection des tapisseries de Louis XIV* (Dijon: Faton, 2010).

10 Ibid., no. 12, p. 307, and no. 70, p. 348.

11 Barbara Brejon de Lavergnée, *Dessins de Simon vouet 1590–1649* (Paris: Réunion des Musées Nationaux, 1987).

12 Louis Demonts, "Les amours de Renaud et Armide, décoration peinte par Simon Vouet pour Claude de Bullion," *Bulletin de la Société de l'Histoire de l'art français* (Paris, 1913): 58–78.

13 Vittet et al., *La collection des tapisseries de Louis XIV*, p. 40, no. 13, and p. 58, no. 21 (or no. 1, p. 295).

14 Maurice Fenaille et al., *Etat-Général des tapisseries de la manufacture des Gobelins, depuis l'origine jusqu'à nos jours*, vol. 1, *Période Louis XIV, 1662–1699* (Paris: Imprimerie Nationale, 1903).

Catalogue

Set of Ten Tapestries (cats. 1–10)
The Story of Rinaldo and Armida

French (Paris), made in the Faubourg Saint-Germain tapestry workshop on rue de la Chaise (active 1633–1667/68) under the direction of Raphaël de La Planche (active there 1633–1661, died 1662) after the designs painted in 1631 by Simon Vouet (1590–1649, *premier peintre du roi*, or first painter to the king, from 1627)

Woven circa 1633–37

Wool and silk; modern cotton lining

See p. 84 for provenance and bibliography for *The Story of Rinaldo and Armida* tapestry cycle

Opposite: Detail of cat. 1.

The tapestry entries are listed here in narrative order, in accordance with the associated canto and verse in Edward Fairfax's English translation of 1600 of the 1581 literary text *Gerusalemme Liberata* by Torquato Tasso (1544–1595) (see the pages following cats. 3, 4, 5, 7, and 10 for Fairfax's translation of the relevant verses). Each entry includes the title of the episode depicted in the tapestry together with the numbers of the canto and verse followed by the identities of the allegorical figures in the borders' cartouches (positioned at the top, left, right, bottom, respectively; or, in the case of the *entrefenêtres*, top and bottom), and the dimensions, woven marks, and accession number.

Armida About to Kill the Sleeping Rinaldo

Canto XIV, verses 64–66

Figures in the border cartouches: Fortitude, Justice, Calliope, Mars

14 ft. 9 in. x 10 ft. 5 in. (449.6 x 317.5 cm)

Woven mark: P + fleur-de-lis + R

Gift of Viola E. Bray, 2005.124.1

The compositions of the tapestries take up Tasso's story of the First Crusade, which, at this point, departs from any semblance of historical fact. Armida, the Saracen princess, has contrived a way to lure the Christian knight Rinaldo off his path and away from his companions to an enchanted place where the air is gentle and cool. He is lulled into a deep sleep by the melodious song of a siren. This tapestry shows the arrival of Armida upon the scene, ready to murder the defenseless knight with a knife. She is stayed in the act, however, when she gazes upon his face, peaceful in repose, and finds herself beguiled by his masculine beauty. Despite her anger and disdain, she falls in love with his recumbent form. A supporting cast of characters helps to tell the tale: winged Zephyr, god of the gentle west wind, hovers in the air with the siren, who points to the sleeper with a rod, while an armed Cupid kneels on the ground below, aiming his arrow at Armida (fig. 1–1). *CB-D*

Fig. 1–1. Detail of cat. 1

Rinaldo Carried to Armida's Enchanted Chariot

Canto XIV, verse 68

Figures in border cartouches: Mercury, Justice, Navigation (or the Sciences), Minerva

14 ft. 9 in. x 14 ft. 3 in. (449.6 x 434.3 cm)

Woven mark: P and to the right, fleur-de-lis + R

Gift of Viola E. Bray, 2005.124.2

Having decided to spare the life of Rinaldo, the princess transports the knight to her palace on an enchanted island located far beyond the western horizon. The island is invisible to common mariners and defended by fantastical, fierce monsters. To reach that destination, Armida uses a chariot that flies through the air, drawn by horses (or by dragons, according to the poem). This tapestry shows the slumbering knight, bound by garlands of flowers, being lifted into the conveyance. A small, ornamental part of the gilded chariot—the carved figurehead of a female with plaited and upswept hair—is just visible behind the tree at right, protruding somewhat awkwardly from the trunk.[1] Grasping the tall stem of a sunflower, Armida is aided by an attendant and four putti (fig. 2–1). The symbolism of the sunflower, placed so prominently in the center of the composition, remains uncertain, although it may allude to the westward direction she will take in her chariot. Like the heliotropic flower, she will follow the sun as it travels west through the sky toward the famed Pillars of Hercules (the promontories that flank the straits of modern-day Gibraltar).[2] *CB-D*

Fig. 2–1. Detail of cat. 2

1   The full design of Armida's golden chariot is revealed in wider versions of the scene. See, for instance, the example bearing the arms of François Petit de Villeneuve (d. 1705, a councilor at the *Cour des Aides*) and Marie-Anne de Foucault, now in the Cummer Museum of Art, Jacksonville, Florida, gift of Eunice Pitt Odom Semmes (formerly in the collection of the marquis de Lareinty-Tholozan at the château de Guermantes, sold (as *The Story of Achilles*) Hôtel Drouot, Paris, December 19, 1917, lot 111; subsequently Jack Chrysler/Mrs. Garbisch [Jack Forker Chrysler 1912–1958 was the younger brother of Bernice Chrysler Garbisch, 1907–1979]; by September 1940, French & Company, New York, stock 19842 and image GCPA 0242289 (at http://piprod.getty.edu/starweb/psc/servlet.starweb) or that in the collection of the Fondation Toms Pauli, Lausanne, Switzerland, inventory number 56. See Guy Delmarcel et al., *The Toms Collection: Tapestries of the Sixteenth to Nineteenth Centuries*, ed. Giselle Eberhard Cotton and trans. Irena Podleska and Geoffrey Peek (Lausanne, Switz.: Fondation Toms Pauli and Zurich and Sulgen, Switz.: Niggli, 2010), cat. no. 54, pp. 160–65.

2   Sunflowers are native to South America and first reached Europe in the early sixteenth century. They were recorded in European botanical treatises from the mid 1500s, where the flowers were admired for their height, but images of them do not appear in the visual arts until about 1620, when they began to be included in floral still lifes. The sunflower in "Rinaldo Carried to Armida's Enchanted Chariot" reflects Vouet's awareness of its novelty in art. For an entry on the sunflower (the "marigold of Peru") in a botanical treatise contemporary with *The Story of Rinaldo and Armida*, see John Gerard, *The Herbal or General History of Plants: The Complete 1633 Edition as Revised and Enlarged by Thomas Johnson* (London, 1633; New York: Dover Publications, reprint edition, 1975), book 2, chapter 259, p. 751.

Armida Driving Her Chariot

Canto XIV, verse 68 or, possibly, canto XVI, verses 69–70

Figures in border cartouches (there are no side borders in this *entrefenêtre*): Fortitude, Prudence

15 ft. 1 in. x 6 ft. 3 in. (459.7 x 190.5 cm)

Woven mark: P + fleur-de-lis + R

Gift of Viola E. Bray, 2005.124.3

The French term *entrefenêtre* (literally, "between window") refers to a tapestry designed to hang in the space between two windows on an interior wall. The specific subject of this narrow *entrefenêtre* has not been confirmed with any precision in the historical records that deal with the production of this series. Given the resemblance of Armida's dress and the carved details of her chariot to the corresponding elements in the preceding tapestry, it is possible that the subject here continues the same scene and represents "Armida Driving Her Chariot" to the enchanted island. Alternatively, the subject may represent a later moment in the story when Armida, abandoned by Rinaldo, flies back to the Holy Land whipping her horses in a fit of fury and revenge. *CB-D*

Translation of Tasso's *Jerusalem Delivered* for cats. 1–3

1. Armida About to Kill the Sleeping Rinaldo

Canto XIV
verse 64

[*Spoken by an old wizard to the knights,
quoting the false words of a singing sprite*]
"But let your happy souls in joy possess
The ivory castles of your bodies fair,
Your passed harms salve with forgetfulness,
Haste not your coming evils with thought and care,
Regard no blazing star with burning tress,
Nor storm, nor threatening sky, nor thundering air,
This wisdom is, good life, and worldly bliss,
Kind teacheth us, nature commands us this."

verse 65

"Thus sung the spirit false, and stealing sleep,
To which her tunes enticed his heavy eyes,
By step and step did on his senses creep,
Still every limb therein unmoved lies,
Not thunders loud could from this slumber deep,
Of quiet death true image, make him rise:
Then from her ambush forth Armida start,
Swearing revenge, and threatening torments smart."

verse 66

"But when she looked on his face awhile,
And saw how sweet he breathed, how still he lay,
How his fair eyes though closed seemed to smile,
At first she stayed, astound with great dismay,
Then sat her down, so love can art beguile,
And as she sat and looked, fled fast away
Her wrath, that on his forehead gazed the maid,
As in his spring Narcissus tooting laid."

2. Rinaldo Carried to Armida's Enchanted Chariot

3. Armida Driving Her Chariot

Canto XIV
verse 68

"Of woodbines, lilies, and of roses sweet,
Which proudly flowered through that wanton plain,
All platted fast, well knit, and joined meet,
She framed a soft but surely holding chain,
Wherewith she bound his neck his hands and feet;
Thus bound, thus taken, did the prince remain,
And in a coach which two old dragons drew,
She laid the sleeping knight, and thence she flew."

Opposite: Detail of cat. 3

Carlo and Ubaldo at the Fountain of Laughter

Canto XV, verses 57–66

Figures in border cartouches: Urania, Victoria, Navigation (or the Sciences), Prudence

14 ft. 9 in. x 12 ft. 7 in. (449.6 x 383.5 cm)

Woven mark: fleur-de-lis + R

Gift of Viola E. Bray, 2005.124.4

Meanwhile, Godfrey de Bouillon (leader of the Christian crusaders) notes the absence of Rinaldo and sends the knights Carlo and Ubaldo in search of him. Forewarned by an all-knowing mystic, the mysterious Hermit Peter, the two of them hear of Rinaldo's abduction and learn how they can rescue him. Hermit Peter, who is not portrayed in the tapestry cycle, equips the knights with a magic scepter and an indestructible shield of adamant made with diamonds. This tapestry moves several episodes ahead in the story in the quest to recover Rinaldo. Carlo and Ubaldo have reached the enchanted island of Armida in a boat guided by Fortune, have already fought a guardian monster, and are now confronting the temptation posed by the nymphs at the fountain of laughter (fig. 4–1). Bathing in the pool of water, the lovely females encourage the men to refresh themselves at the table of food nearby and to drink from the fountain water. Thanks to the counsel of Peter and the protective force of the scepter, the two knights are able to pass by and avoid the peril of that water, which renders the drinker eternally helpless in a fit of endless laughter. *CB-D*

Fig. 4–1. Detail of cat. 4

Translation of Tasso's *Jerusalem Delivered* for cat. 4

4. Carlo and Ubaldo at the Fountain of Laughter

Canto XV
verse 57

"See here the stream of laughter, see the spring,"
Quoth they, "of danger and of deadly pain,
Here fond desire must by fair governing
Be ruled, our lust bridled with wisdom's rein,
Our ears be stopped while these Sirens sing,
Their notes enticing man to pleasure vain."
Thus passed they forward where the stream did make
An ample pond, a large and spacious lake.

verse 58

There on a table was all dainty food
That sea, that earth, or liquid air could give,
And in the crystal of the laughing flood
They saw two naked virgins bathe and dive,
That sometimes toying, sometimes wrestling stood,
Sometimes for speed and skill in swimming strive,
Now underneath they dived, now rose above,
And ticing baits laid forth of lust and love.

verse 59

These naked wantons, tender, fair and white,
Moved so far the warriors' stubborn hearts,
That on their shapes they gazed with delight;
The nymphs applied their sweet alluring arts,
And one of them above the waters quite,
Lift up her head, her breasts and higher parts,
And all that might weak eyes subdue and take,
Her lower beauties veiled the gentle lake.

verse 60

As when the morning star, escaped and fled
From greedy waves, with dewy beams up flies,
Or as the Queen of Love, new born and bred
Of the Ocean's fruitful froth, did first arise:
So vented she her golden locks forth shed
Round pearls and crystal moist therein which lies:
But when her eyes upon the knights she cast,
She start, and feigned her of their sight aghast.

verse 61

And her fair locks, that in a knot were tied
High on her crown, she 'gan at large unfold;
Which falling long and thick and spreading wide,
The ivory soft and white mantled in gold:
Thus her fair skin the dame would clothe and hide,
And that which hid it no less fair was hold;
Thus clad in waves and locks, her eyes divine,
From them ashamed did she turn and twine.

verse 62

Withal she smiled and she blushed withal,
Her blush, her smilings, smiles her blushing graced:
Over her face her amber tresses fall,
Whereunder Love himself in ambush placed:
At last she warbled forth a treble small,
And with sweet looks her sweet songs interlaced;
"Oh happy men I that have the grace," quoth she,
"This bliss, this heaven, this paradise to see."

"This is the place wherein you may assuage
Your sorrows past, here is that joy and bliss
That flourished in the antique golden age,
Here needs no law, here none doth aught amiss:
Put off those arms and fear not Mars his rage,
Your sword, your shield, your helmet needless is;
Then consecrate them here to endless rest,
You shall love's champions be, and soldiers blest."

"The fields for combat here are beds of down,
Or heaped lilies under shady brakes;
But come and see our queen with golden crown,
That all her servants blest and happy makes,
She will admit you gently for her own,
Numbered with those that of her joy partakes:
But first within this lake your dust and sweat
Wash off, and at that table sit and eat."

While thus she sung, her sister lured them nigh
With many a gesture kind and loving show,
To music's sound as dames in court apply
Their cunning feet, and dance now swift now slow:
But still the knights unmoved passed by,
These vain delights for wicked charms they know,
Nor could their heavenly voice or angel's look,
Surprise their hearts, if eye or ear they took.

For if that sweetness once but touched their hearts,
And proffered there to kindle Cupid's fire,
Straight armed Reason to his charge up starts,
And quencheth Lust, and killeth fond Desire;
Thus scorned were the dames, their wiles and arts
And to the palace gates the knights retire,
While in their stream the damsels dived sad,
Ashamed, disgraced, for that repulse they had.

Carlo and Ubaldo Spy on the Lovers

Canto XVI, verses 17–20

Figures in border cartouches:
Mercury, Justice, Navigation
(or the Sciences), Minerva

14 ft. 11 in. x 16 ft. 5 in.
(454.7 x 500.4 cm)

Woven mark: P + fleur-de-lis + R

Gift of Viola E. Bray, 2005.124.5

In this tapestry, the two dauntless companions have gotten past the guards of Armida's palace and discover in its garden the spellbound Rinaldo languishing indolently in the arms of the princess. No longer dressed in armor, nor bearing a sword, the emasculated Rinaldo holds up a mirror for Armida as she binds her hair with a string of pearls. Putti attend the couple as Carlo and Ubaldo (hidden in the trees at left) see that the knight has forgotten entirely the call to arms. Armida's hand mirror provides a visual clue to his predicament (see fig. 5-1), as its frame is modeled with a pair of sirens whose beautiful upper torsos distract the eye from their true deceitful nature, which is only revealed in their coiling tails below (see fig. 6–1). *CB-D*

Fig. 5–1. Detail of cat. 5

Translation of Tasso's *Jerusalem Delivered* for cat. 5

5. Carlo and Ubaldo Spy on the Lovers

Canto XVI

verse 17

Through all this music rare, and strong consent
Of strange allurements, sweet 'bove mean and measure,
Severe, firm, constant, still the knights forthwent,
Hardening their hearts gainst false enticing pleasure,
'Twixt leaf and leaf their sight before they sent,
And after crept themselves at ease and leisure,
Till they beheld the queen, set with their knight
Besides the lake, shaded with boughs from sight:

verse 18

Her breasts were naked, for the day was hot,
Her locks unbound waved in the wanton wind;
Some deal she sweat, tired with the game you wot,
Her sweat-drops bright, white, round, like pearls of Ind;
Her humid eyes a fiery smile forthshot
That like sunbeams in silver fountains shined,
O'er him her looks she hung, and her soft breast
The pillow was, where he and love took rest.

verse 19

His hungry eyes upon her face he fed,
And feeding them so, pined himself away;
And she, declining often down her head,
His lips, his cheeks, his eyes kissed, as he lay,
Wherewith he sighed, as if his soul had fled
From his frail breast to hers, and there would stay
With her beloved sprite: the armed pair
These follies all beheld and this hot fare.

verse 20

Down by the lovers' side there pendent was
A crystal mirror, bright, pure, smooth, and neat,
He rose, and to his mistress held the glass,
A noble page, graced with that service great;
She, with glad looks, he with inflamed, alas,
Beauty and love beheld, both in one seat;
Yet them in sundry objects each espies,
She, in the glass, he saw them in her eyes.

Opposite: Detail of cat. 5

Rinaldo Views His Image in the Diamond Shield

Canto XVI, verses 29–31

Figures in the border cartouches: Urania, Justice, Calliope, Mars

14 ft. 11 in. x 12 ft. 8 in. (454.7 x 386.1 cm)

Woven mark: R + fleur-de-lis

Gift of Viola E. Bray, 2005.124.6

As instructed by Hermit Peter, the two companions wait for a moment until Rinaldo is alone so that they may confront him without the intervention of the sorceress. At the first opportunity, they approach the dull-witted knight and recall him to his duty by raising the magical diamond shield of adamant before his eyes so that he sees his true reflection. Awakening from his stupor, Rinaldo reacts with embarrassment and shame, as depicted in this tapestry. Lifting his hands in the air, he drops Armida's smaller hand mirror (fig. 6–1) and recovers his senses. *CB-D*

Fig. 6–1. Detail of cat. 6

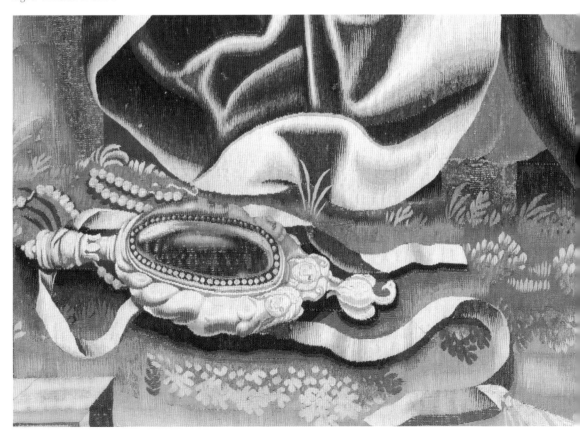

Rinaldo and His Companions Leave the Enchanted Isle

Canto XVI, verses 60–61

Figures in the border cartouches:
Fortitude, Victoria, Calliope, Mars

14 ft. 9 in. x 10 ft. 6 in.
(449.6 x 320 cm)

Woven mark: P + fleur–de–lis + P[1]

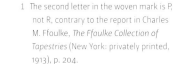

Gift of Viola E. Bray, 2005.124.7

Rinaldo resolves to leave the enchanted island, to return to the crusaders' camp in the Holy Land, to reconcile himself with his captain, and to restore his honor by proving his valor on the field of battle. With Carlo and Ubaldo, he embarks on the boat that brought those two knights to the island. The trio is waylaid by a beseeching and distraught Armida, who begs Rinaldo to stay or, at least, to allow her to follow him. Feeling remorse for her grief, the hero experiences a conflict of emotions, expressed by his glance and hand gesture, but nonetheless departs without her. This tapestry shows the moment when the boat sails past the prostrate princess, who has fallen in a swoon of despair (fig. 7-1). *CB-D*

1 The second letter in the woven mark is P, not R, contrary to the report in Charles M. Ffoulke, *The Ffoulke Collection of Tapestries* (New York: privately printed, 1913), p. 204.

Fig. 7–1. Detail of cat. 7

Translation of Tasso's *Jerusalem Delivered* for cats. 6 and 7

6. Rinaldo Views His Image in the Diamond Shield

Canto XVI
verse 29

> So fared Rinaldo when the glorious light
> Of their bright harness glistered in his eyes,
> His noble sprite awaked at that sight
> His blood began to warm, his heart to rise,
> Though, drunk with ease, devoid of wonted might
> On sleep till then his weakened virtue lies.
> Ubaldo forward stepped, and to him hield
> Of diamonds clear that pure and precious shield.

verse 30

> Upon the targe his looks amazed he bent,
> And therein all his wanton habit spied,
> His civet, balm, and perfumes redolent,
> How from his locks they smoked and mantle wide,
> His sword that many a Pagan stout had shent,
> Bewrapped with flowers, hung idly by his side,
> So nicely decked that it seemed the knight
> Wore it for fashion's sake but not for fight.

verse 31

> As when, from sleep and idle dreams abraid,
> A man awaked calls home his wits again;
> So in beholding his attire he played,
> But yet to view himself could not sustain,
> His looks he downward cast and naught he said,
> Grieved, shamed, sad, he would have died fain,
> And oft he wished the earth or ocean wide
> Would swallow him, and so his errors hide.

7. Rinaldo and His Companions Leave the Enchanted Isle

Canto XVI
verse 60

> Thou closed thine eyes, Armida, heaven envied
> Ease to thy grief, or comfort to thy woe;
> Ah, open them again, see tears down slide
> From his kind eyes, whom thou esteem'st thy foe,
> If thou hadst heard, his sighs had mollified
> Thine anger, hard he sighed and mourned so;
> And as he could with sad and rueful look
> His leave of thee and last farewell he took.

verse 61

> What should he do? leave on the naked sand
> This woeful lady half alive, half dead?
> Kindness forbade, pity did that withstand;
> But hard constraint, alas! did thence him lead;
> Away he went, the west wind blew from land
> Mongst the rich tresses of their pilot's head,
> And with that golden sail the waves she cleft,
> To land he looked, till land unseen he left.

Opposite: Detail of cat. 7

Armida, the Sorceress, Calls Upon the Powers of Magic to Avenge Her Loss

Canto XVI, verses 67–68

Figures in border cartouches (there are no side borders in this *entrefenêtre*): Urania, Prudence

15 ft. 1 in. x 7 ft. 8 in. (459.7 x 233.7 cm)

Woven mark: P + fleur–de–lis + R

Gift of Viola E. Bray, 2005.124.8

This second *entrefenêtre* shows a scene that many have interpreted as "Armida, the Sorceress, Calls Upon the Powers of Magic to Avenge Her Loss" (fig. 8-1). From the despair of her abandonment, the spurned princess quickly succumbs to a fierce rage that demands revenge upon Rinaldo and upon all of the Christian crusaders. She is shown in a fury amidst sparks and a dark cloud that eclipses the sun. She decides to leave the island in order to gather her soldiers and her allies for a climactic battle outside the walls of Jerusalem. She intends to fight the enemy to the death.[1]   *CB-D*

1   Specific details in this scene, such as the open book and staff held by Armida, led Louis Demonts to interpret it as depicting a much earlier moment in the epic, when the sorceress temporarily changed several knights into fish (canto X, verse 65). But, as the outdoor setting of the *entrefenêtre* does not correspond otherwise to this earlier chapter, this interpretation is open to debate. See Louis Demonts, "Les Amours de Renaud et d'Armide," *Bulletin de la Société de l'Histoire de l'Art Français* (Paris, 1913): 61–62.

Fig. 8–1. Detail of cat. 8

Armida Flees the Field of Battle

Canto XX, verse 121

Figures in border cartouches (there are no side borders in this *entrefenêtre*): Fortitude, Mars

14 ft. 11 in. x 6 ft. 1 in. (454.7 x 185.4 cm)

Woven mark: R[1]

Gift of Viola E. Bray, 2005.124.9

The last two tapestries bring *The Story of Rinaldo and Armida* to its conclusion and, with it, the epic poem. Both present scenes that occur after the great battle, which the crusaders have won despite the overwhelming number of Saracen and allied forces. The victory is due in no small part to the courageous Rinaldo, who, driven to restore his honor, fights in a frenzy of blood lust until all his opponents are dead. Seeing the defeat and destruction of her troops, Armida rides away in shame. This third and last *entrefenêtre* of the set shows the armor-clad princess riding side-saddle on a horse, pursued by a Cupid who chastises her with whips made from strings of pearls (fig. 9–1). *CB-D*

1 There is an old repair, immediately to the left of the R, that may have replaced part of the original mark.

Fig. 9–1. Detail of cat. 9

Rinaldo Prevents the Suicide of the Despairing Armida

Canto XX, verse 127

Figures in border cartouches:
Urania, Victoria, Calliope,
Prudence

14 ft. 8 in. x 10 ft. 4 in.
(447 x 315 cm)

Woven mark: P+ fleur-de-lis + R

Gift of Viola E. Bray, 2005.124.10

Alone and overcome with grief and loss, a defeated and spurned Armida attempts suicide with an arrow to her chest. In "Rinaldo Prevents the Suicide of the Despairing Armida," this fatal action is arrested by Rinaldo, who spied her departure from the battlefield and followed in pursuit. Stirred by compassion, he seeks reconciliation with her and, motivated by this generosity of spirit on his part, Armida converts to Christianity. Just before her death, which comes nevertheless, she bequeaths her crown and wealth to him. This ultimate victory of conversion and redemption is celebrated by the putto who flies in from above, carrying a palm frond (fig. 10–1). *CB-D*

Fig. 10–1. Detail of cat. 10

Translation of Tasso's *Jerusalem Delivered* for cats. 8, 9, and 10

8. Armida, the Sorceress, Calls Upon the Powers of Magic to Avenge Her Loss

Canto XVI
verse 67

When she came home, she called with outcries shrill,
A thousand devils in Limbo deep that won,
Black clouds the skies with horrid darkness fill,
And pale for dread became the eclipsed sun,
The whirlwind blustered big on every hill,
And hell to roar under her feet begun,
You might have heard how through the palace wide,
Some spirits howled, some barked, some hissed, some cried.

verse 68

A shadow, blacker than the mirkest night,
Environed all the place with darkness sad,
Wherein a firebrand gave a dreadful light,
Kindled in hell by Tisiphone the mad;
Vanished the shade, the sun appeared in sight,
Pale were his beams, the air was nothing glad,
And all the palace vanished was and gone,
Nor of so great a work was left one stone.

9. Armida Flees the Field of Battle

Canto XX
verse 121

This done, Rinaldo stayed and looked around,
Where he should harm his foes, or help his friends;
Nor of the Pagans saw he squadron sound:
Each standard falls, ensign to earth descends;
His fury quiet then and calm he found,
There all his wrath, his rage, and rancor ends,
He called to mind how, far from help or aid,
Armida fled, alone, amazed, afraid.

10. Rinaldo Prevents the Suicide of the Despairing Armida

Canto XX
verse 127

And with that word half mad, half dead, she seems,
An arrow, poignant, strong and sharp she took,
When her dear knight found her in these extremes,
Now fit to die, and pass the Stygian brook,
Now prest to quench her own and beauty's beams;
Now death sat on her eyes, death in her look,
When to her back he stepped, and stayed her arm
Stretched forth to do that service last, last harm.

Provenance and bibliography for *The Story of Rinaldo and Armida* tapestry cycle (cats. 1–10)

Provenance: The set of ten tapestries ordered about 1633 by Jules Mazarin (1602–61, cardinal from 1641 and chief minister of France from 1642) from the Raphaël de La Planche tapestry workshop in the Faubourg Saint-Germain; Cardinal Antonio Barberini (1607/08–71, cardinal from 1627), purchased December 12, 1637 for the price of 2,760 *écus* and taken to his residence, "Casa Grande" (Palazzo Barberini alle Quattro Fontane), Rome, by 1639, where they were displayed not chronologically but spatially as permitted by the dimensions of the walls in two rooms, seven of them in the former audience hall of his elder brother Cardinal Francesco Barberini (1597–1679, cardinal from 1623) and three of them in a bedchamber.[1] Temporarily hung in the Jesuit Church of Il Gesù, Rome, October 2, 1639.[2] By descent to Carlo Barberini (1630–1704, cardinal from 1653), Palazzo Barberini alle Quattro Fontane, Rome, inventoried on October 25, 1695.[3] By descent through the Barberini Family, Palazzo Barberini alle Quattro Fontane, Rome, until 1889 when sold by the "Princess Barberini," possibly Anna Barberini-Colonna di Sciarra of Palestrina (1840–1911) or her sister Luisa Barberini-Colonna di Sciarra of Palestrina (1844–1906); Charles Mather Ffoulke (1841–1909), Washington, D.C., 1889; Mrs. Hamilton McKown Twombly (born Florence Vanderbilt, 1854–1952), "Florham Farm Estate," Convent (between Morristown and Madison), New Jersey, by 1913, where they were displayed in the Great Drawing Room.[4] By descent to her daughter, Ruth Vanderbilt Twombly (1885–1955), and sold after her death at an auction on the premises of "Florham" in Convent, New Jersey, conducted by Parke-Bernet Galleries, Inc., June 15–16, 1955, lots 493–502. Acquired at that sale by Antiquities, Inc., a subsidiary of French & Company, New York; French & Company, New York, before March 31, 1956, stock number 56038-X; purchased December 26, 1959 by Viola E. Bray (1873–1961), Flint;[5] gifted to Flint Board of Education in 1961 (housed at the FIA), transferred ownership to FIA in 2005.

Bibliography: Ffoulke 1913, pp. 203–13; Demonts 1913, pp. 58–78; Fenaille 1923, vol. 1, pp. 319–35, esp. p. 325; Hunter 1925, pp. 142–43; Ffoulke 1930; "Coming Auctions," *Art News* 1955, p. 66; Crelly 1962, pp. 104–6, 171, 205, illustrating the Vouet models as figs. 125–30; Flint 1963; Coural 1967, pp. 15–24 and 68–75, nos. 27–30, pp. 68–75; Lee 1967, pp. 48–56; Hoff 1971–72, pp. 25–29; Standen 1973, pp. 91–97, esp. p. 95 and note 5 on p. 97; Flint 1979, pp. 4–7; Lavalle 1990, pp. 489–503, 512–18; Thuillier et al. 1990, pp. 116–18; Denis 1996, pp. 143–89; Bertrand 2000, pp. 154–66, ill'd. figs. 3, 4, 10; Bertrand 2005, pp. 118–22, note 63 on p. 190, and notes 209–39 on pp. 181–84 and ill'd. figs. 121–24, 126; Unglaub 2006, pp. 3, 62–70, and notes 10 on p. 228, and 55 on p. 236, and ill'd. fig. 21 on p. 67; Denis 2007, pp. 129–30 and notes 42–43 on p. 139; Vittet 2007, pp. 163–69; Delmarcel et al. 2010, cat. no. 54, pp. 160–65; Vittet and Brejon de Lavergnée 2010, pp. 58–59.

Opposite: Detail of cat. 10, showing Victoria

1   Contrary to many reports, the set was not a gift from Louis XIII to Cardinal Antonio Barberini. See Pascal-François Bertrand, "Une esposition de tapisseries à Rome pour le centenaire des Jesuites," *Antologia di Belle Arti (Studi sul Settecento II)* (Turin, Italy), nos. 59–62 (2000): 164. For further details and the proposed distribution of pieces, see Pascal-François Bertrand, *Les tapisseries des Barberini et la decoration d'intérieur dans la Rome baroque* (Turnhout, Belgium: Brepols, 2005), p. 141, note 63 on p. 190, and note 221 on p. 182.

2   At least three from this set of tapestries appear in the 1641 painting *The Visit of Pope Urban VIII to the Church of Il Gesù, Rome on 2 October 1639*, by Andrea Sacchi (1599–1661), Jan Miel (ca. 1599–1664), and Filippo Gagliardi (d. 1659), now in the Museo di Roma, Palazzo Barberini alle Quattro Fontane, Rome.

3   Charles M. Ffoulke, *The Barberini Tapestries: Armida and Rinaldo Series at "Florham," Convent, New Jersey*, ed. and revised by Cushing Stetson (New York: privately printed by J. J. Little & Ives, 1930), p. 47.

4   In 1930, the privately printed monograph about this set noted that some of the tapestries still bore linings inscribed with the name of Cardinal Antonio Barberini and stamped with the initials FB; ibid., p. 10. It is not known when these possibly original, seventeenth-century linings were removed, but they no longer survive. In the 1980s, the tapestries underwent a conservation treatment during which new cotton linings were applied. The 1980s treatment reports in the FIA object file do not mention the presence of any marks or inscriptions on the linings that were removed at that time.

5   French & Company stock sheet no. 56038-X (GRI Research Library, Los Angeles).

Angel

Peter Paul Rubens, Flemish,
1577–1640

1610/11

Oil on canvas

80½ x 57 in.
(204.5 x 144.8 cm)

Gift of Viola E. Bray, 2005.158

Provenance: Church of Saint
Walburga, Antwerp, 1610; purchased
in 1737 by Canon Engelgrave; Baron
de Vinck, Heer van Westwezel;
Jean-Baptiste-Pierre Le Brun, sale,
Paris, April 11, 1791, no. 68; 5th and
6th Marquess of Hertford, Ragley
Hall, Alcester, Warwickshire; sale,
London, May 20, 1938, no. 29
("Rubens: the Archangel Gabriel, in
the clouds, holding a laurel wreath,
81 in. by 59 in."); Dr. Paul Drey, sold
to French & Company, New York,
in 1951; purchased May 30, 1958
by Viola E. Bray (1873–1961), Flint;[6]
gifted to Flint Board of Education in
1961 (housed at the FIA), transferred
ownership to FIA in 2005.

Bibliography: Rooses 1888, p. 74,
no. 281; Evers 1942; Larsen 1952, no.
20, p. 215 (repr. pl. 43); Freemantle
1959, p. 127; Burchard and d'Hulst
1963, p. 95; Flint 1963; Martin
1969, p. 40; Baudouin 1972, pp. 73,
79; Flint 1979, p. 9; Martin 1985,
pp. 141–46; Belkin 1998, cover ill.;
Lawrence 1999, ills. on pp. 275, 287;
Lawrence 2005.

This painting of an angel by Peter Paul Rubens was part of a larger altarpiece commissioned for the no longer extant Church of Saint Walburga in Antwerp. Executed between 1610 and 1611, shortly after Rubens returned to the Netherlands from his eight years of artistic training in Italy, the altarpiece consisted of several different parts, including his well-known large triptych *The Raising of the Cross* (figs. 11–1 and 11-2), which is now in the Antwerp Cathedral. The other pieces of the altarpiece included three predella paintings (small panels at the base related to the central scene),[1] two cut-out panel angels, a painting of God the Father, and a gilt-wood pelican sculpture. The altarpiece was dismantled in the early eighteenth century, never to be fully restored to its original appearance, and the ancillary paintings, including the FIA's *Angel*, were sold to raise money for a new altar.[2] The angel in Flint is one of two pieces recovered from this dismantling; the other piece is one of the predella panels, which is now in the Museum der bildenden Künste in Leipzig.[3] The angel in Flint originally surmounted the altarpiece (about 35 feet from the ground), flanking a painting of God the Father (present location unknown), and was meant to be seen at a distance from below, as if in flight.[4] In addition to the laurel wreath of victory, the angel once held a palm in his right hand, possibly made of metal.[5]

Fig. 11–1. Peter Paul Rubens, *The Raising of the Cross* (open position) with side panels *The Virgin and St. John with Women and Children and Roman Soldiers*, 1610/11; oil on panel, central panel: 181⅞ x 118⅛ in. (462 x 300 cm); side wings, each: 181⅞ x 59 in. (462 x 150 cm). Antwerp Cathedral. Photo © KIK–IRPA, Brussels

Fig. 11–2. Peter Paul Rubens, *Saints Amandus, Walburga, Elgius, and Catherine* (exterior of wings of fig. 11–1). Antwerp Cathedral. Photo © KIK–IRPA, Brussels

When Rubens's *Angel* entered the FIA collection on a rectangular canvas (fig. 11–3), its original location was known, but perhaps not its original appearance as a cut-out panel painting.[7] When concerns over changes in the paint surface[8] necessitated the painting's removal in 1974 to a conservation laboratory in Oberlin, Ohio,[9] an interesting discovery was made: at some date in its history, the figure of the angel had been transferred from a wood panel to a canvas, and only part of the painting was originally on this wood surface. X-rays of the painting revealed wood-grain patterns on the canvas, but only in the figure area, not in the area of the sky surrounding the angel. Although transferring a painting from a wood surface to canvas was not an unusual practice (the procedure was often believed to be necessary to preserve the paint surface), what was unexpected was that this wood surface was found to exist beneath only part of the painting. One possible explanation for this anomaly was discovered during both curatorial and conservation research, which was being conducted concurrently:[10] the work in the Flint collection was originally a shaped (i.e., cut-out) panel painting, one of only two known surviving examples of painted cut-out figures designed by Rubens (the other being a cut-out panel depicting Juno and Jupiter, now in the Koninklijk Museum voor Schone Kunsten in Antwerp).[11] A painting showing the altarpiece while it still stood in the Church of Saint Walburga provides visual evidence for this original location and appearance (fig. 11–4; the FIA's *Angel* is in the upper left section next to a painting of God the Father).

The condition of the painting was closely examined to determine what original paint remained and whether or not steps should be taken to restore the painting to the way the artist intended. The first of many painstakingly slow and careful steps was to remove all the overpaint and varnish (see figs. 11–5 and 11–6).[12] Often when paintings suffer losses of paint due to age or climate conditions, these areas are filled in or overpainted to make the painting look complete. When all the overpaint was removed on the Rubens *Angel* it was discovered that more than 80 percent of the original paint remained. Because so much of the original work by the artist existed, conservators decided to transfer the painting back to a panel shaped like its original. However, rather than transfer it back to wood, which would have created future problems, the conservators at Oberlin used an aluminum honeycomb-core panel that would be sturdy enough to support the painting and flexible enough to accommodate climate changes.[13]

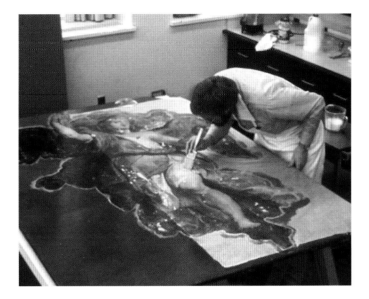 

Fig. 11–5. During conservation process, before removal from canvas. Photo: Intermuseum Laboratory, Oberlin, Ohio

Fig. 11–6. During conservation process, fastening edge to panel. Photo: Intermuseum Laboratory, Oberlin, Ohio

The restoration process, which included inpainting minor losses, was completed in October 1978 (four years after the painting entered the laboratory) with a highly successful result. Not only is this work one of only two surviving examples of Rubens's shaped panels, but it was also most likely done entirely by Rubens without the assistance of workshop painters. Its style exhibits the influences of the Italian artists that Rubens studied, such as Michelangelo, Titian, and Caravaggio. *TJG*

1   The panels are as follows: *The Removal of the Body of St. Catherine by Angels, The Miracle of St. Walburga,* and *Christ on the Cross;* see John Rupert Martin, "The Angel from Rubens's 'Raising of the Cross,'" in *Rubens and His World,* ed. Roger Adolf d'Hulst (Antwerp: Het Gulden Cabinet, 1985), p. 141.
2   Ibid.
3   *The Miracle of St. Walburga in a Storm at Sea;* see Martin, "The Angel from Rubens's 'Raising of the Cross,'" p. 142. The location of the other pieces is currently unknown.
4   Ibid., p. 143. For more information about how the altar's original placement and lighting was taken into consideration by Rubens, see Cynthia Lawrence, "Before *The Raising of the Cross:* The Origins of Rubens's Earliest Antwerp Altarpieces," *Art Bulletin* 81, no. 2 (June 1999): 279 and 287.
5   Martin, "The Angel from Rubens's 'Raising of the Cross,'" p. 143. French & Company stock sheet no. 8005 (GRI Research Library, Los Angeles) describes this work as an angel of martyrdom.
6   French & Company stock sheet no. 8005 (GRI Research Library, Los Angeles); see also Martin, "The Angel from Rubens's 'Raising of the Cross,'" note 6 on p. 142.

7   According to French & Company stock sheet no. 8005, this work was definitively by Rubens; but at some point before the Flint 1963 publication, its authorship was doubted, because it was changed to "attributed to Rubens." Erik Larsen, in a letter to G. Stuart Hodge, August 30, 1968 (in FIA curatorial file 2005.158), pointed out that this work is "one of the best documented Rubens paintings in this country," and that the painting should be considered as wholly by Rubens. The letter was apparently written after Larsen saw the painting at the Wichita Art Institute exhibition *Masterpieces of Religious Art* (December 1, 1967–January 30, 1968). Hodge, in a letter to William Richards, Viola Bray's son-in-law, September 3, 1968 (in FIA curatorial file 2005.158), said that he could not recall how or why the Rubens's attribution was doubted.
8   French & Co. correspondence in FIA curatorial file 2005.158 also indicates that conservation was done on this painting in the spring of 1968: Marguerite Coffey (secretary, French & Co.) to G. Stuart Hodge, March 5, 1968; Hodge to Mitchell Samuels (co-founder, French & Co.), March 1968; Samuels to Hodge, n.d.

9   See FIA curatorial file 2005.158.
10 Richard Spear, conservator at Oberlin, and Pearson Marvin, assistant curator at the FIA, were following the same trail regarding the painting's original location and shape, which John Martin, Princeton University, confirmed, according to correspondence in FIA curatorial file 2005.158: Marvin to Martin, February 28, 1974; G. Stuart Hodge to Marigene Butler (director, Oberlin laboratory), March 1, 1974; Marvin to Butler, March 4, 1974; Martin to Marvin, March 11, 1974.
11 Martin, "The Angel from Rubens's 'Raising of the Cross,'" p. 146.
12 See correspondence in conservation file in FIA curatorial file 2005.158: treatment records kept by Intermuseum Laboratory, Oberlin, Ohio.
13 Martin, "The Angel from Rubens's 'Raising of the Cross,'" p. 143.

Wine Cistern

Workshop of Orazio Fontana
(ca. 1510–1576), Urbino

ca. 1565–75

Tin-glazed earthenware

14 x 22 in.
(35.6 x 55.9 cm)

Gift of Viola E. Bray, 2005.155

Provenance: Possibly Marquis
of Linlithgow (d. 1908); Spanish
Art Gallery, London; purchased
August 18, 1930 by French & Co.,
New York;[5] purchased May 30,
1958 by Viola E. Bray (1873–1961),
Flint; gifted to Flint Board of
Education in 1961 (housed at the
FIA), transferred ownership to FIA
in 2005.

Bibliography: Detroit 1958, p. 42
no. 138; Flint 1963; Flint 1979, pp.
8–9.

Made in Orazio Fontana's workshop (known for its tin-glazed earthenware, called maiolica),[1] this wine cistern may be related to a large set known as the Spanish Service, commissioned by Guidobaldo della Rovere, duke of Urbino (1514–74) between 1560 and 1562, as a gift to Philip II of Spain (1527–98). While no piece from this set for Philip II has been identified conclusively,[2] we know that all of them were decorated with scenes from the life of Julius Caesar,[3] as is the one in Flint, which depicts a naval battle. In 1562, shortly after the Spanish Service was completed, one observer remarked, "[I]n it one might study the arts of sculpture, painting, and illumination or miniature, as well as the history of Caesar."[4]

In the scene painted on the interior of the basin, warriors with helmets, shields, spears, and swords fight each other in ships near the coastline. Some warriors have fallen to their deaths in the water; others struggle to help comrades who have fallen overboard back

into the boat. In the background of the battle scene, civilians have gathered to watch the violence from the shore, standing amidst classical architecture. The battle depicted is not an actual battle but rather a staged version put on by Julius Caesar to celebrate his military victories. In 46 B.C., after winning several key battles during the Civil War, Caesar staged a series of triumphs in Rome to commemorate his victories in Gaul, Africa, Pontus (present-day northeastern Turkey), and Spain.[6] According to the Greek historian Appian of Alexandria, "He gave also various spectacles with horses and music, a combat of foot-soldiers, 1,000 on each side, and a cavalry fight of 200 on each side. There was also another combat of horse and foot together. There was a combat of elephants, twenty against twenty, and a naval engagement of 4,000 oarsmen, where 1,000 fighting men contended on each side."[7]

This depiction of Caesar's naval-battle triumph has been identified as having been done after a drawing by Mannerist painter Taddeo Zuccaro (1529–1566) (fig. 12–1).[8] That this work and its related versions were based on designs by Zuccaro indicates its importance, as most maiolica works were not based on specifically made designs by painters.[9] It is thought that Zuccaro's drawings were used by maiolica painters until about 1585.[10] Besides the scene painted on the basin's interior, the decorations painted on this wine cistern also includes *grotteschi* (grotesques), lion's-head and -paw supports, and antique swags. Recent research suggests that these grotesque designs were derived from *Les Petites Grotesques* (published in 1550 and 1562), which featured etchings by French architect and designer Jacques I Androuet du Cerceau (1510–1584) (figs. 12–2, 12–3).[11] Many images on the Flint cistern can be found in *Les Petites Grotesques*, including figures standing on dolphinlike creatures, bird beasts with serpents' tails, squatting figures supporting medallions, and musical instruments in juxtaposition with weaponry (figs. 12–4, 12–5).

Orazio Fontana came from an important family of potters in Urbino, Italy, who were known for their white-ground maiolica decorated with *istoriato* (narrative scenes inspired by classical literature, history, and religious or mythological texts) and grotesques. Starting off as a painter of *istoriato* ceramics, Orazio eventually, at age fifty-five, founded his own workshop in Urbino, producing ceramics for the Medici family in Florence, among others. His nephew Flaminio continued the family business until the late sixteenth century.[12]

In addition to its aesthetic presence, this cistern had a practical use: when the vessel was filled with cold water, wine bottles were set in it to be kept chilled. *TJG*

Fig. 12–4. Detail of cat. 12

Fig. 12–5. Detail of cat. 12

1 Timothy Wilson attributes pieces related to the FIA wine cistern to the Fontana family because they show similarities to it but lack Orazio's signature; Timothy Wilson, *Italian Maiolica of the Renaissance* (Milan: Bocca, 1996), p. 372.

2 Charlotte Vignon, *Exuberant Grotesques: Renaissance Maiolica from the Fontana Workshop* (New York: Frick Collection, 2009), p. 25. Wilson mentions that the lack of a coat of arms where it would be expected seems to indicate that no pieces have survived from the Spanish Service; Wilson, *Italian Maiolica*, p. 372.

3 J. A. Gere, "Taddeo Zuccaro as a Designer for Maiolica," *Burlington Magazine* 105, no. 724 (July 1963): 306. For more on the iconography see Wilson, *Italian Maiolica*, p. 372, and Vignon, *Exuberant Grotesques*, p. 36.

4 Quoted in Gere, "Taddeo Zuccaro as a Designer," note 5 on p. 306.

5 French & Company stock sheet no. 37254 (GRI Research Library, Los Angeles) notes that the cistern was from the collection of the Marquis of Linlithgow.

6 Wilson, *Italian Maiolica*, p. 372 and note 12 on p. 376.

7 Appian, *The Civil Wars* (2.102).

8 The drawing "after" Zuccaro in the British Museum (1895,0915.652) shows the same battle scene; the original Zuccaro drawings are not extant (see Vignon, *Exuberant Grotesques*, p. 26). For a list of the nine drawings (copies) of this scene, see Gere, "Taddeo Zuccaro as a Designer," note 15 on p. 309. Gere mentions that the popularity of this scene is indicated by the number of extant copies.

9 Related versions with the same naval battle scene (but with different borders) include cisterns in: Bargello, Florence; Museo Nazionale di Capodimonte, Naples; Prado, Madrid (0457), which depicts a similar naval battle but on a different cistern shape; a 1950 Parke-Bernet sale (see Wilson, *Italian Maiolica*, note 4 on p. 376); and Wallace Collection, London (C107). Vignon, referring to this work, wrote: "Paolo Mario of Urbino noted in a letter dated September 17, 1562: 'I have found that more care has been taken over the making of that earthenware service than if it had been made of precious stones. The drawings were brought here from Rome, drawing by drawing, by the hand of a celebrated painter, who has with the greatest skill and effort depicted all the history and deeds of Julius Caesar'"; Vignon, *Exuberant Grotesques*, pp. 25–26; letter also quoted in Gere, "Taddeo Zuccaro as a Designer," p. 306.

10 Wilson, *Italian Maiolica*, p. 375.

11 Vignon, *Exuberant Grotesques*, p. 27; see also Christopher Poke, "Jacques Androuet I Ducerceau's 'Petites Grotesques' as a Source for Urbino Maiolica Decoration," *Burlington Magazine* 143, no. 1179 (June 2001): 332–44.

12 Wendy M. Watson, "Fontana," *Oxford Art Online*.

Cat. 13a

Cat. 13b

Pair of Vases

13.

Style of Fontana family

Late 16th century

Each 15½ x 11 in.
(39.4 x 27.9 cm)

Tin-glazed earthenware

Inscribed "CHRISTOFAN DE VRB(ino)[?]"[1]

Gift of Viola E. Bray, 2005.157.1–2

Provenance: Alessandro Castellani (1823–83), Paris, by 1877, nos. 294–95;[4] French & Company, New York; purchased May 30, 1958 by Viola E. Bray (1873–1961), Flint; gifted to Flint Board of Education in 1961 (housed at the FIA), transferred ownership to FIA in 2005.

Bibliography: Beckwith 1877, p. 68; Flint 1963.

This pair of maiolica vases is decorated in the style of Orazio Fontana (ca. 1510–71), whose workshop in Urbino was known for creating the kind of white-ground grotesques and *istoriato* scenes that are seen here.[2] Maiolica (also spelled majolica) refers to tin-glazed earthenware produced during the Italian Renaissance. The term was originally used to describe Hispano-Moresque ceramics imported to Italy from the island of Majorca (at one time called Isola di Majolica) that inspired Italian potters during the sixteenth century.

During the Renaissance, tin-glazed maiolica was prized for its white color emulating Chinese porcelain valued by European collectors. This white glaze, *bianco*, was a mixture of lead and tin oxides applied after the earthenware vessel was shaped and fired. Once dry, painters used metallic oxide colors, such as cobalt blue, manganese purple and brown, copper green, antimony yellow, and iron orange, to create images against the white ground. Painting the earthenware in colors was a very difficult task, because all the paints appeared light gray or beige before firing. The bright colors of the paint were not visible before the work was fired, requiring craftsmen to imagine how the images would look on the fired piece; and once it was fired, the painter could not make any changes to the final product.

On this white background, the Fontana workshop painted *istoriato* (narrative scenes inspired by classical literature, history, and religious or mythological texts). Surrounding these scenes were *grotteschi* (grotesques; see explanation at entry no. 12). Works like these were often used to display the family's wealth and status, displayed on a *credenza* in a prominent place in the living area.[3]

Each vase shows two different scenes (see figs. 13–1, 13–2). One vase depicts the mythological scene of Danaë and the shower of gold (pictured opposite, cat. 13a). In several myths, the king of the gods, Zeus (Jupiter in Roman mythology), disguises himself to have sexual relations with mortal women; in this scene he has become a shower of gold. After a prophecy predicted that Danaë's future son would kill her father, he locked up his daughter in a bronze tower so that she would remain childless. Nevertheless, Zeus visited Danaë as a shower of gold during her imprisonment and impregnated her. She bore the hero Perseus, who, as the prophecy foretold, killed his grandfather. The opposite side of this vase shows the Judgment of Paris (fig. 13–2), the legendary contest where Paris, the handsome Trojan prince, must choose which of three goddesses is the most beautiful. He awards the golden apple to Venus, goddess of love, over Juno (Hera in Greek mythology) and Minerva (Athena), after Venus promised him Helen of Troy, the most beautiful woman in

Opposite: Fig. 13–1. Detail showing
back of cat. 13b

Above: Fig. 13–2. Detail showing
back of cat. 13a

the world. Paris's action was said to launch the Trojan War. Both scenes, set in medallions, are surrounded by white-ground grotesques and putti. Male, bearded masks surmount serpentlike handles, with female masks below them.

The other vase shows the allegorical figure of Justice (cat. 13b), holding a sword, with the inscription "GIVSTIZIA." The other side depicts Neptune, Roman god of the sea, riding a hippocamp, a horse with a fishlike hindquarter (often called a sea-horse) (fig. 13–1). Each scene is set in an architectural niche surround by white-ground grotesques. On the Justice side, two putti grasp the Corinthian columns supported by lions. On the Neptune side, bearded telamons (male figures that serve as columnar supports) flank the central scene. The niche is supported at the base by dolphins, which are attributes of Neptune. As in the other vase, male and female masks adorn the handles and sides.

The shape of both vases is modeled after ancient Greek or Roman vessels. *TJG*

1 Last word blurred. "DE URB(ino)" is listed as the inscription in the 1877 and 1878 publications cited in note 4 below.
2 Charlotte Vignon, *Exuberant Grotesques: Renaissance Maiolica from the Fontana Workshop* (New York: Frick Collection, 2009), p. 9.
3 Ibid., p. 10.
4 Arthur Beckwith, *Majolica and Fayence: Italian, Sicilian, Majorcan, Hispano-Moresque and Persian* (New York: D. Appleton, 1877), p. 68; *Catalogue des Faiences Italiennes*, auction catalogue at Hôtel Drouot, May 27–28, 1878, nos. 294–95.

Deruta Maiolica Vase

Italian

16th century

Tin-glazed earthenware

14 x 12 x 12 in.
(35.6 x 30.5 x 30.5 cm)

Gift of Viola E. Bray, 2005.156

Provenance: Possibly Howard
I. Pratt, New York; French &
Company, New York; purchased
May 30, 1958 by Viola E. Bray
(1873–1961), Flint; gifted to Flint
Board of Education in 1961 (housed
at the FIA), transferred ownership
to FIA in 2005.

Bibliography: Flint 1963.

This vase of tin-glazed earthenware (called maiolica) was made in Deruta, a town in Italy that has manufactured pottery since the Middle Ages. In the early sixteenth century, Deruta ceramics were produced with a metallic luster surface, a technique inspired by Islamic and Hispano-Moresque pottery.[1] Compounds containing silver or copper were painted on the fired pottery, which was then refired at a lower temperature. Distinguished by their use of yellow and pearly luster, Deruta ceramics are also known for their restricted color schemes and clear decorative patterns.[2] The two-dimensional designs on this vase (fig. 14–1), which cover the whole surface except for trim bands of solid yellow at the lip and base, work well with its simple shape and smooth contours. *TJG*

1 Alan Caiger-Smith, *Tin-Glaze Pottery*
   (London: Faber and Faber, 1973), p. 93.
2 Ibid., pp. 97–98.

Fig. 14–1. Detail of cat. 14

Cat. 15a

Cat. 15b

Pair of Angels Holding Candlesticks

Giovanni Buora, Italian,
ca. 1450–1513

Late 15th, early 16th century

Sandstone

Each, 39 x 14 x 10 in.
(99 x 35.6 x 25.4 cm)

Gift of Viola E. Bray, 2005.146.1–2

Provenance: Possibly Walter S.
M. Burns, Hatfield, Hertfordshire,
England; Clarence H. Mackay
(1874–1938), New York, by about
1920;[4] French & Company, New
York; purchased May 30, 1958 by
Viola E. Bray (1873–1961), Flint;
gifted to Flint Board of Education in
1961 (housed at the FIA), transferred
ownership to FIA in 2005.

Bibliography: Flint 1963.

This pair of sandstone angels, dating from the late fifteenth to early sixteenth century, may have been part of a larger sculpted group in a church interior not yet identified. The candlesticks, held in opposite hands by each angel, may have been a later addition, as there is evidence of them having been broken off and repaired at some point in the angels' history.[1] The square plinth they stand on may also be a later addition.[2] Only the front and sides are carved, suggesting that they were not meant to be seen in the round. Although the figures are angels, they are depicted without wings. The clinging drapery, naturalistic pose, and graceful features of these angels all are influences of the naturalism favored in ancient Greek and Roman art, which was revived during the Renaissance.

Originally attributed to Venetian sculptor Pietro Lombardo, these angels have recently been reassigned to Giovanni Buora, an architect and colleague of Pietro.[3] Most sculptors during the High Renaissance in Venice also worked for family businesses who, like the Lombardo family, were known to have employed stonecutters and sculptors for architectural projects. Buora worked on several well-known projects, including the church of San Zaccaria, the Scuola Grande di San Marco, and San Giorgio Maggiore. *TJG*

1   Ann Markham Schulz, Brown University,
    e-mail to Tracee Glab, Flint Institute of
    Arts, April 18, 2010.
2   Alison Luchs, National Gallery of Art,
    Washington, D.C., e-mail to Tracee Glab,
    Flint Institute of Arts, April 1, 2010.

3   FIA curatorial file 2005.146.1–2; and
    e-mails from Alison Luchs and Ann
    Markham Schulz to Tracee Glab (see
    notes 1 and 2 above). Note that a similar
    pair of limestone angels attributed to
    the workshop of Buora were sold at
    Christie's by the Columbus Museum
    of Art in November 2010 (sale 2360).
    See Ann Markham Schulz, "One Old,
    and Nine New, Attributions to Giovanni
    Buora," *Rivista d'Arte* (new series)
    no. 1 (2011).

4   A photograph of Mackay's music room
    at Harbor Hill, Roslyn, New York, taken
    in about 1920 shows the sculptures
    on white pedestals flanking a window;
    Charlotte Vignon, *Exuberant Grotesques:
    Renaissance Maiolica from the Fontana
    Workshop* (New York: Frick Collection,
    2009), p. 19; and French & Company
    provided a typed description to the FIA,
    which notes that they were no. 19 in the
    Mackay collection catalogue (1926) (in
    FIA curatorial file 2005.146.1–2).

Youthful Martyr Saint

Italian (possibly Florentine)

15th century

Terracotta, polychromed

27 x 16 x 9½ in.;
H. of modern base: 4 in.
(68.6 x 40.6 x 24.1 cm)

Gift of Viola E. Bray, 2005.152

Provenance: French & Company, New York; purchased May 30, 1958 by Viola E. Bray (1873–1961), Flint; gifted to Flint Board of Education in 1961 (housed at the FIA), transferred ownership to FIA in 2005.

Bibliography: Flint 1963.

Although we know some things about this sculpture, its exact origin, artist, and identity remain a mystery. Her style of dress and head covering can be seen in other works of the mid-fifteenth century (e.g., Fra Filippo Lippi's *The Annunciation*, ca. 1450–53; National Gallery of Art, London). The palm offers a clue to her identity, as it was often included in a work of art to indicate someone who died as a martyr. Once associated with military victory, the palm was used by the Christian church as a symbol of victory over death.[1] Which martyr saint this sculpture represents remains unknown, however, as there are no other identifying attributes.[2]

This sculpture was originally a full-length, almost life-size figure. At some point in its history, before it entered the Flint collection, the work was broken in half, or possibly detached from its lower half, as large terra-cotta works were often cast in multiple pieces.[3] In the past, this figure of a woman has been attributed to the sculptor Desiderio da Settignano, known for his graceful depictions of women and children in early Renaissance Florence.[4] The similarities between the Flint work and confirmed works by Desiderio—such as simplicity in dress, smoothness and roundness of shoulders, gaping mouth to display emotion, and an elongated, elegant neck—suggest that the sculptor of the Flint work most likely knew something of the Desiderio style. *TJG*

1   Cesare Ripa, *Baroque and Pictorial Imagery: The 1758–60 Hertel Edition of Ripa's* Iconologia *with 200 Engraved Illustrations*, ed. Edward A. Maser (New York: Dover, 1971), no. 50, "Truth," and no. 140, "Reward."

2   For a discussion on female saints in Italian Renaissance art, see Paola Tinagli, *Women in Italian Renaissance Art: Gender, Representation, Identity* (Manchester: Manchester University Press, 1997), pp. 155–84.

3   Bruce Boucher, ed. *Earth and Fire: Italian Terracotta Sculpture from Donatello to Canova* (New Haven: Yale University Press, 2001), pp. 91–93. The paint on the terra-cotta of the FIA work only covers the front, which may suggest that it originally stood in a niche or against a wall in a church or other sacred space.

4   FIA curatorial file 2005.152. For more on Desiderio, see Marc Bonnard et al., eds. *Desiderio da Settignano: Sculptor of Renaissance Florence*, exh. cat. (Washington, D.C.: National Gallery of Art, 2007).

Figure of an Angel

17.

Attributed to Giovanni della
Robbia, Italian, 1469–1529

Late 15th, early 16th century

Tin-glazed earthenware

26 x 9 x 9 in.
(66 x 22.8 x 22.8 cm)

Gift of Viola E. Bray, 2005.153

Provenance: Possibly Empress
Frederick (Victoria, 1840–1901,
consort of Frederick III, Emperor
of Germany; daughter of
Queen Victoria), Friedrichshof,
Kronberg; Baron Maximilian von
Goldschmidt-Rothschild (1843–
1940), Frankfurt; Rosenberg and
Stiebel; purchased April 6, 1953
by French & Company, New York;[4]
purchased May 30, 1958 by Viola
E. Bray (1873–1961), Flint; gifted
to Flint Board of Education in 1961
(housed at the FIA), transferred
ownership to FIA in 2005.

Bibliography: Detroit 1958, p. 73;
Flint 1963; Flint 1979, p. 10.

This figure of an angel has been attributed to Giovanni della Robbia, a grandnephew of
Luca della Robbia (1399/1400–1482), a Florentine sculptor credited with the invention of
applying tin glazes to terra-cotta to create a dazzling white surface. Luca's experimentation
with ceramic glazing in early-fifteenth-century Florence was very successful, and the objects
created in his workshop were in demand for several years.[1] The special tin-glaze recipe was
kept a secret within the Della Robbia family, with Luca's nephew Andrea (Giovanni's father)
continuing the business. Della Robbia objects were known for their white figures against a
blue background, with Madonna and Child subjects being the most desirable.[2]

   This angel was created using the same technique that the Della Robbia name was known
for. Tin-glazed earthenware became extremely popular
because of its beauty and durability, costing much less
than marble, stone, or bronze sculpture. The Della Robbia
workshop created a wide range of works in this medium,
including church furnishings, altarpieces, family shields,
floor and ceiling tiles, and private devotional sculpture.
Giovanni, trained by his father, eventually abandoned the
pure white surface in works executed between 1510 and
1529, preferring to use vivid polychrome glazes on later
works.[3] *TJG*

Side view of cat. 17

1   Francesca Petrucci, Giancarlo Gentilini,
    and Fiamma Domestici, *Della Robbia*
    (Milan: Giunti, 1999), p. 5.
2   Ibid., p. 11.
3   Allan Marquand, *Giovanni della Robbia*
    (Princeton: Princeton University Press,
    1920), pp. xiii–xv.

4   French & Company stock sheet no.
    53085 (GRI Research Library, Los
    Angeles) includes the following: "From
    the Collection of Baron Max von
    Goldschmidt-Rothschild, Frankfort.
    Formerly in the Collection of Empress
    Frederick, Castle Friedrichshof,
    Cronberg."

Pair of Altar Candlesticks

Attributed to Giuseppe de Levis, Italian, 1552–1611/14

Late 16th, early 17th century

Bronze

Each, H. 32½ in., base 10 in. (H. 82.55 cm, base 25.4 cm)

Gift of Viola E. Bray, 2005.147.1–2

Provenance: William Randolph Hearst (1863–1951); purchased December 7, 1951 by Clendenin J. Ryan, New York;[5] purchased April 16, 1952 by French & Company, New York; purchased May 30, 1958 by Viola E. Bray (1873–1961), Flint; gifted to Flint Board of Education in 1961 (housed at the FIA), transferred ownership to FIA in 2005.

Bibliography: Flint 1963.

Opposite: Cat. 18a (left) and cat. 18b (right)

These bronze candlesticks were part of a set designed for an altar that included a matching crucifix.[1] Designed to hold one candle each, the candlesticks would have been used during the celebration of the Catholic Mass or Eucharist. From at least the thirteenth century, candles were placed on the altar, one on each side of the cross. On certain religious occasions, more than two candlesticks would have been used.[2] These types of candlesticks were not intended for domestic or ordinary use but reserved for sacred settings only.

Attributed to the sculptor and bronze-founder Giuseppe de Levis, from Verona, this set features female grotesque figures and putti arranged in tiers among urns, leaves, and scrolling motifs. The tiers are topped by a plinth bearing an acanthus-leaf candleholder. Giuseppe specialized in decorative arts, including inkstands, doorknockers, andirons, and church bells.[3] During the sixteenth century, bronze sculptors often made their work in another medium, such as terra-cotta, then giving it to a bronze-founder to execute their design. In Giuseppe's case, he had expertise in both design and the fabrication process and executed his own work.[4] *TJG*

1 Similar (but not identical) candlesticks are in the Lehman Collection, Metropolitan Museum of Art, New York (nos. 1975.1.1403–1404), attributed to circle of Alessandro Vittoria (1525–1608); and in the Saint Louis Art Museum (nos. 1339 and 1340), acquired January 8, 1926, with provenance of Raoul Heilbroner, attributed to Paduan school. Thus, there are a total of six candlesticks that look similar to one another (including the FIA set) and to a crucifix at the Phoenix Museum of Art.

2 "Altar Candlesticks," *The Catholic Encyclopedia* (1913), p. 350.

3 Peta Motture, ed., *Large Bronzes in the Renaissance* (New Haven, Conn.: Yale University, 2003), p. 278.

4 Ibid., p. 279. See also Charles Avery, "Levis [Levi], Giuseppe [Joseph] de," *Oxford Art Online*, where it is noted that Giuseppe's confirmed works are typically signed, "IOSEPH DE LEVIS IN VERONA MI FECE"; the bronze candlesticks in the Flint's collection described here do not have an inscription.

5 French & Company stock sheet no. 52192–X (GRI Research Library, Los Angeles) includes what it refers to as "their mark": "207–Hearst sale 1294–12/7/51." It also includes "P.O. 47581 4/25/53" on the same line.

19.

Diana and Apollo

Attributed to Girolamo Campagna,
Italian, 1549–1629

Late 16th, early 17th century

Bronze

Each, 25³/₄ x 10 x 7¹/₂ in.
(65.4 x 25.4 x 19 cm)

Gift of Viola E. Bray, 2005.151.1–2

Provenance: Possibly Baron Eugen
Kohner, Budapest;[4] Ephron Gallery;
purchased November 12, 1953 by
French & Company, New York;
purchased May 30, 1958 by Viola
E. Bray (1873–1961), Flint; gifted
to Flint Board of Education in 1961
(housed at the FIA), transferred
ownership to FIA in 2005.

Bibliography: Flint 1963; Flint 1979,
p. 10.

Opposite: Bronze sculpture of
Diana (cat. 19a)

This pair of bronze sculptures depicts the Roman gods Diana and Apollo, who were twin siblings. Their parents were Jupiter, ruler of the gods, and Latona, daughter of the Titan Coeus (Zeus and Leto in Greek mythology). According to the myth, Latona was in labor for nine days and nights with the twins and had to flee to a remote area (because of the jealousy of Juno [Hera], Jupiter's wife) to give birth. Diana and Apollo loved their mother a great deal, often resorting to violence to defend her. In one episode, they killed Niobe's seven sons and seven daughters to punish her for boasting that she was superior to Latona.[1]

Diana is shown here as the Roman goddess of the hunt, holding her bow and in the act of drawing an arrow from the quiver on her back. In ancient Greece, she was known as Artemis and was associated with hunting and wild beasts.[2] Earlier, she was also worshiped as an earth goddess who protected animals, tame and wild. Later, she became identified with Luna, the moon goddess, and she was also worshiped by the Romans as a triple deity: Luna, Diana (the earth), and Hecate (the underworld).[3] The composition of this *Diana* was inspired by an ancient Greek sculpture of the goddess, which was copied many times (for example, the Roman copy after a Greek original, *Artemis with a Doe*, in the Musée du Louvre).

Apollo, Roman god of the sun, is depicted with his head turned to the right and about to play his lyre. He also carries a quiver, an allusion to the story that he slew the serpent Python with a thousand arrows, making him the patron of archery. Apollo was also the patron of poetry and music, which is suggested by the lyre he holds (ancient poetry was always sung). Known for his beauty, he had love affairs with several nymphs and mortal women.[5]

The animated poses and twisting motion of this pair of figures anticipate the Baroque style of the seventeenth century. They are attributed to Girolamo Campagna, one of the most important sculptors working in Venice during the late sixteenth and early seventeenth century.[6] In addition to several church commissions in marble and bronze, he also executed public monuments for Venetian doges (chief magistrates). Although he is known mostly for his religious figures, he did produce some works depicting mythological subjects, but they are very rare. Campagna only started working in bronze in 1590, and made several important bronze sculptures between that year and 1593, when he returned to working mostly in marble. He did not return to bronze until 1606.[7] *TJG*

Opposite: Bronze sculpture of Apollo (cat. 19b)

1 Pierre Grimal, *The Dictionary of Classical Mythology*, trans. A. R. Maxwell-Hyslop (Oxford and New York: Blackwell, 1986), p. 257.
2 Ibid., p. 61.
3 James Hall, *Dictionary of Subjects and Symbols in Art* (London: J. Murray, 1974; New York: Harper & Row, 1974, paperback edition), p. 101.
4 French & Company stock sheet no. 54035 (GRI Research Library, Los Angeles) notes that Leo Planiscig illustrates two sculptures similar to

these in the Berlin Museum (signed by Campagna) and notes that others like the ones in Berlin exist in the collections of the National Museum, Munich, Baron Eugen Kohner, Budapest, and the Museo Correr, Venice; see Leo Planiscig, *Venezianische Bildhauer der Renaissance* (Vienna: A. Schroll, 1921). The Flint sculptures of Diana and Apollo were given the Kohner provenance by French & Co. (see FIA curatorial file 2005.151.1–2).

5 Grimal, *Dictionary of Classical Mythology*, pp. 47–50.
6 See Paola Rossi, *Girolamo Campagna* (Verona: Vita Veronese, 1968).
7 Bruce Boucher, "Campagna, Girolamo [Gerolamo]," *Oxford Art Online*.

Figure of the Magdalene

20.

Vincent Nanques, French,
17th/18th century

late 17th/early 18th century

Olive wood

16 x 38 x 17 in.
(40.6 x 96.5 x 43.2 cm)

Gift of Viola E. Bray, 2005.150

Inscribed: NANQUIE FESIT

Provenance: Possibly the office
of Philip IV of Spain (r. 1621–65);
Marquis of Salamanca (1811–83),
Madrid, Spain; Dr. John E. Stillwell
(1853–1930), New York;[6] French
& Company, New York; purchased
May 30, 1958 by Viola E. Bray
(1873–1961), Flint; gifted to Flint
Board of Education in 1961 (housed
at the FIA), transferred ownership
to FIA in 2005.

Bibliography: Flint 1963.

Prior to the 1570s, the New Testament figure of Mary Magdalene was usually depicted as a richly attired, beautiful woman holding the jar of ointment she used to anoint Christ's feet. During the Counter-Reformation, she was represented more frequently as a penitent sinner, dressed in humble clothing, usually with a skull nearby,[1] an image often used by the Catholic Church to encourage devotion to the sacrament of penance. In this figure, the sculptor has included all the elements of her penance: a coarse basket-weave gown with heavy chain, a scourge with six-pointed star, a cross to contemplate Christ's sacrifice, and a skull as a memento mori.

The image of Mary Magdalene was based on three women from the New Testament, including the unnamed prostitute who anointed the feet of Jesus.[2] In the late sixteenth century, artists emphasized her repentance, or turning away from a sinful life. According to the medieval text *The Golden Legend*, which recounted the lives of the saints, Mary lived the rest of her days in a cave in Marseilles. In this legend, she had no food or water, but was sustained for thirty years through daily trips to heaven, where she was given spiritual nourishment.[3] The sculptor has evoked the setting of this cave by including the stony support on which she reclines.

While we know a lot about the subject of this sculpture because of her frequent depictions in art, we know very little about the sculptor who made it. The signature "NANQUIE FESIT [*sic*]" is carved into the left back of the sculpture, on the rock that supports Mary Magdalene. From a nineteenth-century dictionary of French sculptors, we know that a Vincent Nanques, probably from Amiens, married Marie-Catherine Le Gendre, daughter of sculptor Jacques Le Gendre, in 1697 in Paris.[4] No other works by this artist have surfaced, but this style can be seen in other seventeenth-century works.[5] *TJG*

1 See Raymond J. Kelly, III, *To Be, Or Not To Be: Four Hundred Years of Vanitas Painting* (Flint: Flint Institute of Arts, 2006), note 6 on p. 21.

2 Ibid., p. 20.

3 Marjorie M. Malvern, *Venus in Sackcloth: The Magdalen's Origins and Metamorphoses* (Carbondale: Southern Illinois University Press, 1975), pp. 90, 94.

4 "Nanques (Vincent)," Henri Herluison, *Actes d'état-civil d'artistes français peintres, graveurs, architectes, etc.* (Orléans, 1873; Geneva: Slatkine, reprint edition, 1972); "Nanques (Vincent)," Stanilas Lami, *Dictionnaire des sculpteurs de l'école française sous le règne de Louis XIV* (Paris: H. Champion, 1906).

5 For example, *The Penitent Magdalen* (1664) by Nicolas Legendre in the National Gallery of Art, Washington, D.C. (1971.6.1).

6 Typewritten note from French & Company (in FIA curatorial file 2005.150).

Candlestick

Spanish

17th century

Copper-gilt, with blue
enamel plaques

29 x 7 in.
(73.7 x 17.8 cm)

Gift of Viola E. Bray, 2005.148

Inscribed: *guillamas mujer de
ant jomez dio le vera al carmen
mariana de cardenosa*

Provenance: French & Company,
New York; purchased May 30,
1958 by Viola E. Bray (1873–1961),
Flint; gifted to Flint Board of
Education in 1961 (housed at the
FIA), transferred ownership to FIA
in 2005.

Bibliography: Flint 1963; Flint 1979,
p. 12.

Containing four arched niches, with a Christian holy figure in each (fig. 21–1), this seventeenth-century Spanish candlestick was intended for a sacred space. The elaborate shape, adorned with delicate engraving and repoussé ornamentation, shows a range of influences, from the Italian Renaissance to Moorish and Flemish art. Blue enamel plaques accentuate the surface, which is enlivened by cherubs' heads and flowers. The holy figures stand in niches surmounted by classical broken pediments and flanked by Doric columns.

On the base of the candlestick, an inscription is present that may provide a clue to the original whereabouts of this object. Identified as possibly medieval or pre-Enlightenment Castilian, the inscription could perhaps indicate Cardenosa, located in the province of Ávila, Spain, as the original location of either the candlestick's donor or its recipient. *TJG*

Fig. 21–1. Detail of cat. 21

22.

Pair of Andirons

Italian

Late 16th century

Bronze

55 x 21 x 20 in.
(139.7 x 53.3 x 50.8 cm)

Gift of Viola E. Bray, 2005.154.1–2

Provenance: Possibly gift of King Charles IX of France to the Caldora Family; F. Baumeister; purchased May 10, 1919 by French & Company, New York; sold May 12, 1919 to William Randolph Hearst; returned November 30, 1919 to French & Company; sold June 2, 1920 to William Butterworth; his sale at Parke-Bernet Galleries, no. 1540; repurchased October 29, 1954 by French & Company, New York;[3] purchased May 30, 1958 by Viola E. Bray (1873–1961), Flint; gifted to Flint Board of Education in 1961 (housed at the FIA), transferred ownership to FIA in 2005.

Bibliography: Flint 1963.

Opposite: Cat. 22a (left) and cat. 22b (right)

Both functional and decorative, these imposing late-sixteenth-century bronze andirons would have stood within a grand fireplace to support logs for the fire. Cast in separate sections because of their large size, these andirons feature several classically inspired sculpted elements, including grotesque masks (see fig. 22–1), putti, garlands, acanthus leaves, and lions, all surmounted by eagles with the Caldora coat of arms.[1] Said to be a gift from King Charles IX of France (r. 1560–74) to the Caldora family,[2] these andirons depict the French royal arms (with the fleur-de-lis) between the female heads in profile. *TJG*

1   See "Caldora" in Victor Rolland, Johannes Baptist Rietstap, and Henri Rolland, *V. & H. V. Rolland's Illustrations to the Armorial General* (Baltimore: Heraldic Book Co., and London: Heraldry Today, reprint edition, 1967), vol. 1.

2   In an unpublished and undated French & Company ms. (in the FIA curatorial file on the Bray collection): "Armorial andirons which belonged to the Caldora di Napoli e di Nari family of Italy and France. The andirons are surmounted by a spread eagle finial over a lyreform member modeled with nude putti. Two female busts flank an oval escutcheon with the arms of Charles IX of Naples [*sic*], over a base with a central mask and a pair of lions."

3   According to French & Company stock sheets no. 20511 and 55303 (GRI Research Library, Los Angeles): Purchased for $1,000 in 1919; sold to Hearst for $8,250 in 1919; sold to Butterworth for $22,000 in 1920; purchased in 1954 for $250, with firetool set (no. 55304); sold to Bray for $6,500.

Fig. 22–1. Detail of cat. 22b

Armorial Mantelpiece

French

16th century

Stone with traces of
original polychrome

91 x 105 in.
(231.1 x 266.7 cm)

Gift of Viola E. Bray, 2005.159

Provenance: Possibly William
Randolph Hearst (1863–1951);[2]
French & Company. New York;
purchased May 30, 1958 by Viola
E. Bray (1873–1961), Flint; gifted
to Flint Board of Education in 1961
(housed at the FIA), transferred
ownership to FIA in 2005.

Bibliography: Flint 1963.

As the focal point of the room, both as a source of heat and light, fireplaces often received highly decorative mantelpieces. Showing a trace of its original polychrome painting, this sixteenth-century French mantelpiece might have been the chief decorative feature of the room it was in originally. With its elaborately carved details of rinceaux, putti, and engaged Corinthian capitals, and a coat of arms in the center, this imposing work was meant to be noticed by visitors. Two faces in profile, a man and a woman, decorate the side of the mantelpiece. The coat of arms includes (clockwise from top right) the house of Visconti in Milan, the house of Bourbon in France, the Grimaldi of Venice, and the Navarra of Spain (see fig. 23–1).[1] *TJG*

1 Unpublished and undated French
  & Company ms. (in FIA curatorial
  file 2005.159).

2 Typewritten note from French
  & Company (in FIA curatorial file
  2005.159).

Fig. 23–1. Detail of cat. 23, showing coat of arms in the frieze

Cat. 24a

Cat. 24b

Pair of *Cassoni*

Italian

16th century

Walnut, partly gilded

Each, 31 x 77 x 26 in.
(78.7 x 195.6 x 66 cm)

Gift of Viola E. Bray, 2005.125.1–2

Provenance: Possibly Baron
Adolphe de Rothschild, Paris
(1823–1900); inherited by Baron
Maurice de Rothschild (1881–1957),
Paris; Clarence H. Mackay (1874–
1938), New York;[4] purchased April
13, 1948 by French & Company,
New York;[5] purchased May 30,
1958 by Viola E. Bray (1873–1961),
Flint; gifted to Flint Board of
Education in 1961 (housed at the
FIA), transferred ownership to FIA
in 2005.

Bibliography: Detroit 1958, no. 64,
p. 36 (repr. of 2005.125.1, p. 39);
Flint 1963; Flint 1979, p. 15.

Sixteenth-century *cassoni* (chests) were usually commissioned as wedding gifts, taking pride of place in the bedroom, one of the most lavishly furnished rooms in an Italian Renaissance home.[1] Unlike modern-day bedrooms, which are meant to be more private spaces, Renaissance bedrooms had a public function, where visitors were often received and business conducted. As such, the bedroom became an important place to display the family's wealth, status, and unity. These *cassoni* would have served such purposes well. Designed in pairs, and gilded to make parts of the walnut surface look like pure gold, *cassoni* were probably the most expensive items paid out of the wife's dowry by her father.[2] Another indicator that these chests were meant to promote the family's status is the inclusion of two centrally placed coats of arms, each of them set in a cartouche surmounted by eagle heads and held on both sides by angels. The chests' antique-inspired decoration and shape in the form of ancient Roman sarcophagi (stone coffins)[3] would have also reflected the family's taste and cultural refinement.

    The story depicted on these chests is the life of Tobias in eight scenes (four on each chest), based on the apocryphal book of Tobit (father of Tobias). That story would have been appropriate for a newly married couple, as Tobias was rewarded for his faith by being blessed with a wife, Sarah. Two key scenes depicted on one of the chests are their marriage ceremony and wedding night. In the latter, depicted in a contemporary Italian Renaissance interior, with coffered ceiling, fireplace, and bed with drapery, Tobias and Sarah pray for God's blessing, as instructed by the angel. The dog, a symbol of fidelity, is curled up in front of the fire next to the couple (fig. 24–1).

Fig. 24–1. Detail of cat. 24b showing Tobias and Sarah on their wedding night

The other six scenes are from before and after their marriage. The story begins when Tobit, who is blind, sends his son Tobias on a journey to Media to collect money owed to him. Tobias meets a traveling companion, the angel Raphael in disguise. On these chests, Raphael is depicted with wings, but in the story his true angelic identity is concealed from Tobias. During their travels, while Tobias is bathing in the River Tigris a giant fish comes out of the water. Raphael tells Tobias to catch the fish, gut it, and keep the heart, liver, and gall. Later, at the angel's prompting, they stay with Tobias's kinsmen, where he meets Sarah. Even though Sarah has been cursed by a demon, which resulted in the death of seven previous husbands (abducted and killed by the demon on their wedding night before the marriage could be consummated), Tobias marries her, confident in the angel Raphael's protection: the angel has instructed Tobias to burn the heart and liver of the fish during prayer on the wedding night to make the demon flee Sarah. Tobias follows his instructions, thus freeing Sarah from the demonic curse. They return to Tobit as a family, and Tobias uses the fish's gall to heal his father's blindness. The angel Raphael is revealed to all, and they see how they have been blessed by God.

The four scenes on the first *cassone* show the following (from left to right; figs. 24–2 and 24–3): (1) the blessing of Tobit; (2) the angel Raphael, Tobias, and his dog embarking on their journey; (3) Tobias bathing in the River Tigris when a giant fish comes out of the water; (4) Tobias going to stay with his kinsmen. On the second *cassone*, the story continues, showing (from left to right; figs. 24–4 and 24–5): (5) the marriage of Sarah and Tobias; (6) the pair praying on their wedding night; (7) their journey back to Nineveh; (8) the healing of Tobit and the revelation of the angel Raphael's true identity.

Fig. 24–2. Detail of cat. 24a

Fig. 24–3. Detail of cat. 24a

Fig. 24–4. Detail of cat. 24b

Fig. 24–5. Detail of cat. 24b

Fig. 24–6. Detail of cat. 24a   Fig. 24–7. Detail of cat. 24a

On the end panels of these chests, allegorical figures depict the four seasons. Winter is shown as a seated, bearded man warming his hands above a fire, while a winged putto brings him more wood (fig. 24–6). Spring is a reclining nude woman with flowers in her hair, receiving a cornucopia of flowers from a putto (fig. 24–7). Summer is a nude young male laying down and reaching for a basket of fruit, while a winged satyr brings him even more fruit (fig. 24–8). Fall is a semi-draped woman reclining and holding a cornucopia (literally, a horn of plenty) filled with wheat, which is so full and overflowing that a putto has to assist her (fig. 24–9). Perhaps the presence of these allegorical figures on the chests indicates a desire for the married couple to experience happiness and fruitfulness in all seasons.

In addition to these scenes, there are other carvings decorating the chests. The lids are raised panels molded in palmettes and supported by a decorative band of acanthus leaves. Between the palmettes and scrolled vines are youthful masks, with a lion's-mask lock escutcheon in the center, and two draped female figures form the corners. The bases are composed of repeated female masks connected by swags of fruit and flowers. Below the bases are alternating angel's masks with wings, lion's masks, and shallow vases. Each chest rests on four lion's-paw feet. *TJG*

Fig. 24–8. Detail of cat. 24b

Fig. 24–9. Detail of cat. 24b

1 Elizabeth Currie, *Inside the Renaissance House* (London: Victoria and Albert Museum, 2006), pp. 47–49.

2 See Peter Thornton, *The Italian Renaissance Interior, 1400–1600* (London: Weidenfeld and Nicolson, 1991), pp. 192–204.

3 For more on sarcophagus-shaped chests with elaborate carving, see V&A 7708 and 7709–1861 in Marta Ajmar-Wollheim and Flora Dennis, eds., *At Home in Renaissance Italy*, exh. cat. (London: Victoria and Albert Museum, 2006), p. 121.

4 Typewritten note in FIA curatorial file 2005.125.1–2 indicates that this work is cited in the Mackay collection catalogue (1926), no. 35.

5 French & Company stock sheet no. 57311, old no. 79743 (GRI Research Library, Los Angeles).

Cat. 25a (above) and cat. 25b (below)

Pair of Parcel-Gilded Cabinets

Italian

Possibly 17th-century
panels, with later additions

Walnut, partly gilded,
with marble

Each 39¹/₂ x 86 x 26 in.
(100 x 218.4 x 66 cm)

Gift of Viola E. Bray, 2005.126.1–2

Provenance: Hollingworth Magniac,
Esq. (1786–1867), Colworth,
Bedford, England;³ French &
Company, New York; purchased
May 30, 1958 by Viola E. Bray
(1873–1961), Flint; gifted to Flint
Board of Education in 1961 (housed
at the FIA), transferred ownership
to FIA in 2005.

Bibliography: London 1892, p. 88,
no. 285; Flint 1963; Flint 1979, p. 15.

Each of these two cabinets depicts a triumphal procession, a grand parade featuring a victorious public figure in a chariot, illustrating the triumphs of sacred and profane (worldly) love. Triumphal processions originated in ancient Rome and were revived as visual images during the Renaissance.[1] In the fourteenth century, Petrarch wrote the allegorical poem *Trionfi* (Triumphs), which included triumphs of love, chastity, fame, time, and death.[2] Petrarch's poem inspired many images of triumphal processions, mostly shown taking place on land. Although the scenes on these two chests may not depict Petrarch's *Trionfi* specifically, they are possibly derived from that source. The chariot of Venus (who represents profane love) is shown in water, while the pope's chariot (representing sacred love) seems to be coming up out of the water onto a rocky shore. Both figures are shown being crowned with wreaths, symbols of their victory.

The first cabinet's central panel depicts Venus in a water chariot pulled by swans (fig. 25–1), which, because of their beauty, were deemed to be attributes of the goddess of love. A flying putto is crowning Venus with a wreath; and another winged figure blows a trumpet, which was also a sign of triumph. She is also attended by nereids (sea nymphs) in the water alongside her chariot.

Fig. 25–1. Detail of cat. 25a

Fig. 25–2. Detail of cat. 25b

Fig. 25–3. Detail of cat. 25b

The second cabinet's central panel depicts the pope seated in a chariot pulled by winged horses (fig. 25–2). Like Venus, he is being crowned with a wreath by a flying putto, and his arrival is heralded by a winged figure blowing a trumpet. Religious figures, including a cardinal and a bishop, accompany the pope's chariot. The pope is dressed in his ecclesiastical finery, wearing the tiara (three-tiered papal crown) that represents the trinity as well as his authority on earth.[4] This same crown can be seen on the Venus panel of the other cabinet, being carried by a sea nymph in front of Venus's chariot (fig. 25–1).

Each cabinet has two additional panels flanking the central triumphal scene. The two panels on the cabinet with Venus both feature a female figure in a rocky landscape with trees: one on the back of an eagle, the other with a pillar and anchor. The pillar and anchor are associated with Fortitude and Hope, respectively.[5] In the two flanking panels on the papal cabinet, two male figures are shown: on one, a youthful male seated on a horse, holding a mirror (fig. 25–3); on the other, a much older man on the back of a cow.

While each cabinet's dynamic, dramatic curved surfaces are characteristic of the Baroque style popular in seventeenth-century Italy—as are the seashell motifs and theatrical gestures of the figures—it has been suggested by some scholars that only the carved panels date from the seventeenth century. The colorful marble tops and the bodies of the cabinets possibly date from the nineteenth century. *TJG*

1   James Hall, *Dictionary of Subjects and Symbols in Art* (London: J. Murray, 1974; New York: Harper & Row, paperback edition, 1979), p. 310.

2   Margaret Ann Zaho, *Imago Triumphalis: The Function and Significance of Triumphal Imagery for Italian Renaissance Rulers* (New York: Peter Lang, 2004), pp. 33, 36.

3   *Catalogue of the Renowned Collection of Works of Art, Chiefly Formed by the Late Hollingworth Magniac, Esq. (known as the Colworth Collection)*, London, 1892, no. 285 on p. 88.

4   George Ferguson, *Signs and Symbols in Christian Art: With Illustrations from Paintings of the Renaissance* (Oxford: Oxford University Press, 1976), p. 160.

5   Hall, *Dictionary of Subjects and Symbols*, p. 247.

Credenza

Italian (Umbria)

16th century

Walnut with bronze

40 x 93 x 28 in.
(101.6 x 236.2 x 71.1 cm)

Gift of Viola E. Bray, 2005.127

Provenance: Possibly Casa Martelli, Florence; French & Company, New York; purchased May 30, 1958 by Viola E. Bray (1873–1961), Flint; gifted to Flint Board of Education in 1961 (housed at the FIA), transferred ownership to FIA in 2005.

Bibliography: Flint 1963.

A *credenza* in sixteenth-century Italy could be used to display the owner's wealth or as evidence of the family's "credentials" (its economic status),[1] such as precious vessels of metal or of expensive stone placed on ornate textiles. This *credenza* is imposing in its own right, with antique-inspired bronze lion's-mask pulls, lion's-paw feet, and eight elaborately carved male and female pillar figures. It has three recessed drawers on top of three doors that open to reveal additional drawers within. This type of furniture would most likely be located in the *sala*, a room often used for dining and other important events. According to scholars, the name *credenza* is taken from the word *credenziere*,[2] the title of the person responsible for making sure the food to be served at special occasions had not been poisoned or contaminated. Later, this type of furniture became associated with the beautiful objects meant to promote the family's wealth and status displayed on top of it.

This particular *credenza* is said to have originally been in the Martelli Palace in Florence,[3] where it may have stood among the works of contemporary art by Florentine sculptors such as Donatello as well as works from ancient Rome that the Martelli are known to have collected. Another work in the FIA collection said to be from the Martelli Palace is the carved library table (cat. 30). *TJG*

1   Peter Thornton, *The Italian Renaissance Interior, 1400–1600* (London: Weidenfeld and Nicolson, 1991), p. 207.

2   Elizabeth Currie, *Inside the Renaissance House* (London: Victoria and Albert Museum, 2006), pp. 34–35.

3   Typewritten note from French & Company (in FIA curatorial file 2005.127).

Cassapanca

Italian (Florence)

16th century

Walnut

39 x 81 x 25½ in.
(99 x 205.7 x 64.7 cm)

Gift of Viola E. Bray, 2005.128

Provenance: Possibly Elia Volpi (1858–1938), Florence;[2] French & Company, New York; purchased May 30, 1958 by Viola E. Bray (1873–1961), Flint; gifted to Flint Board of Education in 1961 (housed at the FIA), transferred ownership to FIA in 2005.

Bibliography: Flint 1963.

A *cassapanca* (chest bench) satisfies the need for both seating and storage in one piece of furniture. Originating in sixteenth-century Florence, this type of storage furniture seems to have been used exclusively there.[1] More than just a functional object, this one has been carefully carved and constructed to reflect the owner's wealth and status, decorated with symmetrical arrangements of exquisitely carved ornaments that exemplify the revival of the art of antiquity during the Renaissance. The back of the bench is punctuated by scrolling at both ends and is topped by a molded and fluted cornice. The scroll motif is repeated in the bench's substantial arms, which are inset with carved floral panels. The front of the bench, below the seat (which is also the chest's lid), is fluted and decorated with rosettes. Below that is a prominent band of scroll design, with a grotesque mask at its center (fig. 27–1). This *cassapanca* probably would have occupied a prominent position in the living area of a wealthy family. Cushions to make the seating more comfortable would have concealed the lid of the chest. TJG

1   See fig. 296 in William Odom, *History of Italian Furniture from the Fourteenth to the Early Nineteenth Century* (New York: Archive Press, reprint 1966), p. 282.

2   Typewritten note from French & Company (in FIA curatorial file 2005.128).

Fig. 27–1. Detail of cat. 27

Octagonal Table

Italian (Tuscany or Umbria)

ca. 1550–80

Walnut

H. 32 in., diam. 53 in.
(H. 81.2 cm, diam. 134.6 cm)

Gift of Viola E. Bray, 2005.140

Provenance: Elia Volpi (1858–1938), Florence; Carl Hamilton, New York; purchased February 2, 1920 by French & Company, New York;[3] sold to Carl Hamilton, November 19, 1920;[4] repurchased January 27, 1930 by French & Company; purchased May 16, 1930 by Clarence Mackay, New York;[5] Gimbel Brothers;[6] repurchased October 25, 1941 by French & Company; purchased May 30, 1958 by Viola E. Bray (1873–1961), Flint;[7] gifted to Flint Board of Education in 1961 (housed at the FIA), transferred ownership to FIA in 2005.

Bibliography: Detroit 1958, no. 55, p. 35; Flint 1963; Flint 1979, p. 11; Koeppe 1994, p. 30.

Italian Renaissance households sometimes contained an *ottangulo* (octagonal table), with or without elaborate decoration, as is evident from its frequent mention in inventories during the sixteenth century.[1] The original owners of this *ottangulo* are not known, but a clue is given by the two coats of arms included in the decoration of the elaborately carved legs that support the table's plain octagonal surface. Not only did this family want their wealth and status to be known through the heraldry, but other symbols on the legs communicated their desire to provide a bountiful table.

The side of each leg (which terminates in a shaggy lion's-paw foot) is different from all the others, resulting in six carvings, all connected by a central theme. On the sides pictured (left to right), a face shown in profile with a scrolling vine emerging from its mouth is next to a leafy scrolled vine. Moving clockwise, the next pair of carvings feature two coats of arms on either side of a coiled snake and an intertwined cornucopia containing vegetables and shafts of wheat (see p. 27 for an image of these legs). The remaining two sides contain ornate carvings of flowers, vines, and fruit. All these symbols were borrowed from ancient Greek and Roman sources to convey the theme of abundance and fertility. A related version of this *ottangulo* is in the Metropolitan Museum of Art, New York, in a somewhat different style and with slightly different carvings. It has been suggested that these two tables may have been intended for the same family, possibly created for a wedding.[2] *TJG*

1   Peter Thornton, *The Italian Renaissance Interior, 1400–1600* (London: Weidenfeld and Nicolson, 1991), pp. 210–11.
2   See Wolfram Koeppe, "French and Italian Renaissance Furniture at the Metropolitan Museum of Art," *Apollo* 138 (1994): 30.
3   French & Company stock sheet no. 22048 (GRI Research Library, Los Angeles) indicates that Hamilton purchased the table from the Volpi sale, no. 498, with the note "not found in cat.," and that French & Company purchased it in 1920 for $3,300.
4   French & Company stock sheet no. 22048/cross ref. no. 39184 (GRI Research Library, Los Angeles) indicates

that they sold the table back to Hamilton, plus 10 percent ($3,630) on November 19, 1920. A memo line (date crossed out and obscured) on another sheet (number not listed) also indicates that they may have sent it or sold it to C. H. Mackay before Hamilton.
5   French & Company stock sheet no. 39184/cross ref. no. 41982 (GRI Research Library, Los Angeles) states that they bought the table back from Hamilton for $7,959.30 in 1930, and sold it to Mackay for $9,000, less 10 percent; there is also a note on this stock sheet, "bought back @ Gimbel for $718.40" (see note 6).
6   Stock sheet no. 41982/cross ref. no. 39184, 22048 (GRI Research Library, Los

Angeles) states that French & Company purchased the table from Gimbel Bros. on October 25, 1941, for $718.40, with a note that it was in the Mackay Collection.
7   Sold to Mrs. Bray $7,500 on May 30, 1958 (stock sheet no. 41982/cross ref. no. 39184, 22048 [GRI Research Library, Los Angeles]).

Refectory Table

Italian

16th century

Walnut

31½ x 144 x 48 in.
(80 x 365.8 x 121.9 cm)

Gift of Viola E. Bray, 2005.141

Provenance: Possibly Vimercati, Verona; [William] Payne Whitney (1876–1927), New York, by 1918;[4] United Distillers of America;[5] purchased June 4, 1953 by French & Company, New York; purchased May 30, 1958 by Viola E. Bray (1873–1961), Flint; gifted to Flint Board of Education in 1961 (housed at the FIA), transferred ownership to FIA in 2005.

Bibliography: Odom 1966, figs. 139–40; Detroit 1958, no. 70, p. 37 (repr. p. 40); Flint 1963.

This refectory table (a long table for a dining hall), measuring twelve feet wide, is the largest piece of furniture in the Bray collection and dominates the center of the gallery as it might have in its original location. It demonstrates the Renaissance taste for the classical past and the desire of its owner to display the family's wealth and importance. In Italy during the fifteenth century, more commonly used tables were plain, without carved decoration, and were covered with an ornate tablecloth.[1] By the sixteenth century, upper-class families commissioned craftsmen to create tables with elaborate carvings inspired by ancient Roman stone tables.[2] This table's end supports, each of which bears the family's coat of arms (fig. 29–1) between two cornucopia volutes on its outward-facing surface, resemble these classical models. A carving of ivy adorns the inward-facing surface of each end support. The richness of the carving and its monumental size indicate that this table would probably have been used in a palace. The coat of arms has been attributed to the Vimercati of Verona.[3] *TJG*

1 Peter Thornton, *The Italian Renaissance Interior, 1400–1600* (London: Weidenfeld and Nicolson, 1991), p. 205.

2 William M. Odom, *History of Italian Furniture from the Fourteenth to the Early Nineteenth Centuries* (Garden City, N.Y.: Doubleday, Page, 1918–19; New York: Archive Press, reprint edition, 1966), p. 168.

3 Mina Gregori, Princeton University, letter to Flint Institute of Arts, October 31, 1968 (in FIA curatorial file 2005.141).

4 Illustrated in Odom, *History of Italian Furniture* (1966 reprint of 1918 edition), figs. 139–40, where it is listed as being in the collection of Payne Whitney.

5 The stock number on the photo in FIA curatorial file 2005.141 matches the number of French & Company stock sheet no. 53658-X (GRI Research Library, Los Angeles), but the stock sheet describes this object as a "large English refectory table" and does not cite the Payne Whitney provenance.

Fig. 29–1. Detail of cat. 29

Library Table

15th century

Light walnut

33 x 90 x 40 in.
(83.3 x 228.6 x 101.6 cm)

Gift of Viola E. Bray, 2005.142

Provenance: Carlo Girard; purchased September 10, 1930 by French & Company, New York; purchased January 16, 1931 by Preston Pope Satterwhite (1867–1948), New York; French & Company, New York;[4] purchased May 30, 1958 by Viola E. Bray (1873–1961), Flint; gifted to Flint Board of Education in 1961 (housed at the FIA), transferred ownership to FIA in 2005.

Bibliography: Detroit 1958, no. 57, p. 36 (repr. p. 40); Flint 1963; Flint 1979, p. 11.

This library table, notable for its elaborately carved legs terminating in lion's-paw feet, is the only piece of furniture in the Bray collection that was once attributed to an artist—and not just any artist, but one of the biggest names in the Renaissance, the sculptor Donatello.[1] That attribution most likely came about because the table was said to have come from the Martelli Palace in Florence, Italy.[2] During the Renaissance, the Martelli family were avid art patrons and held important political positions, loyal to the Medici. Roberto Martelli was a longtime manager of the Medici bank in Rome. According to tradition, Donatello's mother was a servant in the Martelli household, and Roberto took the sculptor Donatello in as a young boy and became his earliest art patron.[3] The Martelli are said to have owned several works by Donatello, some of which he gave to them in gratitude for their kindness to him. However, Donatello's authorship of this table can most likely be ruled out, because only his sculpted works have been confirmed. *TJG*

1   French & Company stock sheet no. 37308/cross ref. no. 41872 (GRI Research Library, Los Angeles) indicates that this table is "Donatellian" and that it was "originally from Cav. Verti Administrator Via degli Speziali, Florence."

2   The French & Company stock sheet lists a different provenance; a typewritten note from the dealer in FIA curatorial file 2005.142 indicates that this table was originally from the Martelli Palace in Florence.

3   Giorgio Vasari, *The Lives of the Painters, Sculptors, and Architects*, trans. Julia Conaway Bondanella and Peter Bondanella (Oxford: Oxford University Press, 1998), p. 147.

4   French & Company stock sheet no. 37308/cross ref. no. 41872 (GRI Research Library, Los Angeles) does not indicate when they purchased this table back from Satterwhite, but this information was on stock sheet no. 41872, which is no longer extant.

Two-Part Cabinet

French or Italian

Possibly 16th century,
period of Francis I
(r. 1515–47)

Walnut

94 x 59 x 23½ in.
(238.8 x 149.9 x 59.7 cm)

Gift of Viola E. Bray,
2005.143

Provenance: Possibly Clarence H.
Mackay (1874–1938), New York;[1]
French & Company, New York;
purchased May 30, 1958 by Viola
E. Bray (1873–1961), Flint; gifted
to Flint Board of Education in 1961
(housed at the FIA), transferred
ownership to FIA in 2005.

Bibliography: Flint 1963; Flint 1979,
p. 13.

Such an imposing piece of furniture, in addition to being useful for storing important items under lock and key, would have been a sculptural work in its own right. This two-part cabinet, with its classically inspired acanthus leaves, garlands, and mythological figures, as well as its distorted figures and fantastical creatures, is thought to demonstrate the style that was popular in the French court of the sixteenth century.

Six male and female herms (pillar figures), with distorted facial features (see fig. 31–1) and exaggerated physiques, flank cabinet doors carved with decorative elements. The two upper doors feature Roman goddesses set in architectural niches. On the upper left, Diana, goddess of the hunt, is depicted with a bow and arrows and a quiver. On the upper right, Minerva, goddess of wisdom and warfare, is shown wearing a helmet and holding a spear and shield with the face of Medusa. Each niche is surmounted by a broken pediment with fruit (possibly pomegranates) and foliage, with grotesque creatures on either side of the goddess. Beneath the niche is a cherub mask with swags of fruit emerging from its mouth. The two bottom doors depict eagle-headed creatures with breasts terminating in foliage on either side of a female mask. The designer also inserted some playful elements into this work: there is a keyhole disguised in the belly of the female pillar figure with crossed arms between the two upper doors, and another keyhole in the pelvic region of the pillar figure below it. Just above the lower doors, two drawers with lions' heads and swags of fruit complete the façade. The sides also contain carved ornaments, with female masks set in scrolled cartouches (fig. 31–2). Projecting bands of ornament at the top, middle, and bottom also unite the upper and lower parts of the cabinet. *TJG*

1 Typewritten note from French
   & Company (in FIA curatorial file
   2005.143).

Fig. 31–1. Detail of cat. 31

Fig. 31–2. Detail of cat. 31
(side panel)

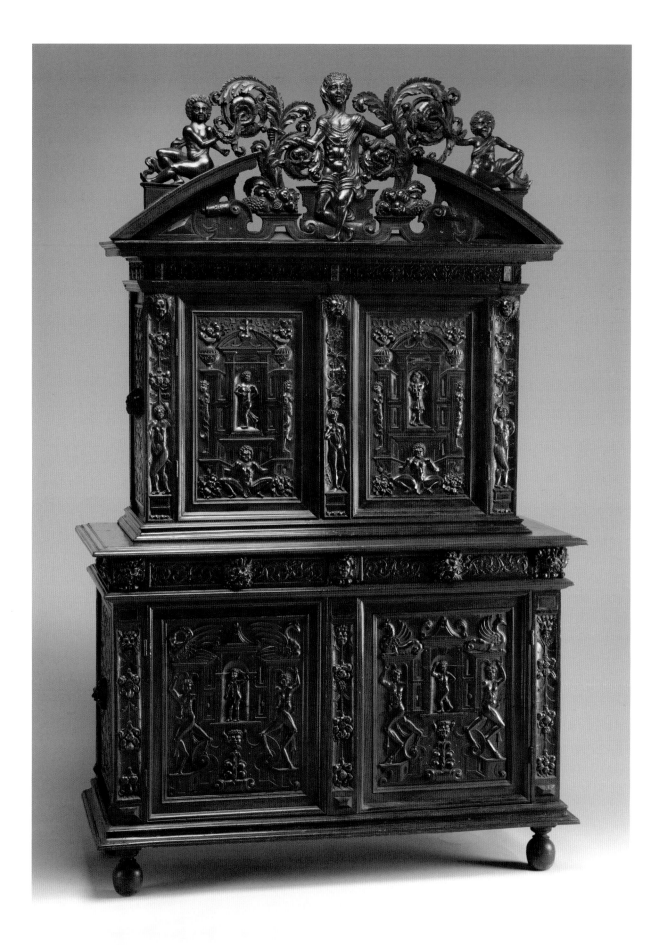

Two-Part Cabinet

32.

French or Italian

16th century, period
of Francis I (r. 1515–47)

Walnut, with lighter wood,
ivory or bone inlay

74 x 55½ x 24 in.
(187.9 x 140.9 x 60.9 cm)

Gift of Viola E. Bray, 2005.144

Provenance: Mrs. Henry Walters,
New York; her sale through A.A.A.
Anderson Gallery; purchased
January 11, 1934 by French &
Company, New York;[2] purchased
May 30, 1958 by Viola E. Bray
(1873–1961), Flint; gifted to Flint
Board of Education in 1961 (housed
at the FIA), transferred ownership
to FIA in 2005.

Bibliography: Flint 1963.

This elaborate two-part cabinet has many striking features but displays an overall harmony of design. Four cabinet doors and two drawer fronts, as well as the cabinet's sides and borders, all bear intricate carving (see figs. 32–1 and 32–2). The bottom part of the cabinet is slightly wider than the top part, and thus serves as a base for it. The top is surmounted by a broken pediment decorated with a prominent sculpture featuring three putti among foliage and fretwork. All four cabinet doors are carved with figures in fantastical architectural niches surrounded by hybrid human figures and perched mythical creatures. The vertical band that separates the two upper cabinet doors also bears a cuirass and shield with a lightning bolt above a female figure holding one breast.

This cabinet, with its two-part form, classically inspired architectural setting, grotesques, vegetal ornaments, distorted figures, and fantastical creatures, is thought to be characteristic of the style that was popular in the French court of the sixteenth century. Made during the reign of Francis I (r. 1515–47), such intricately carved work would have appealed to the French elite.[1] Francis I brought Italian artists and their distinct Mannerist style to his court at Fontainebleau, which influenced French artists. The Mannerist style is characterized by distortion and an element of the bizarre, which is evident in the twisted poses of the figures, some human, some hybrid. *TJG*

1 Alain Gruber, *The History of
   Decorative Arts: The Renaissance
   and Mannerism in Europe* (New York:
   Abbeville Press, 1994), pp. 218–19.

2 French & Company stock sheet no.
   39397 (GRI Research Library, Los
   Angeles) lists this cabinet as "Flemish
   XVI cty."

Fig. 32–1. Detail of cat. 32,
showing cherub on side

Fig. 32–2. Detail of cat. 32, showing
creature on lower right door

Certosina Cabinet

Italian

Late 15th, early 16th century

Walnut and bone or ivory inlay

62½ x 37½ x 15¼ in.
(158.7 x 95.3 x 38.7 cm)

Gift of Viola E. Bray, 2005.145

Provenance: Possibly Davanzati Palace, Florence;[2] Mrs. R. W. Bliss; purchased February 20, 1946 by French & Company, New York;[3] purchased May 30, 1958 by Viola E. Bray (1873–1961), Flint; gifted to Flint Board of Education in 1961 (housed at the FIA), transferred ownership to FIA in 2005.

Bibliography: Flint 1963;[4] Odom 1966, p. 82 (repr. fig. 71); Flint 1979, p. 13.

The dazzling geometric patterns that cover almost every inch of this cabinet are created by a technique known as certosina. Named after the Certosa church in Pavia, Italy, that has an elaborate altarpiece made with this technique,[1] certosina work involves inlaying small pieces of light-colored material—such as bone or ivory—in a dark ground made of wood. Popular during the late fifteenth and early sixteenth centuries in Italy, certosina decoration is thought to have been influenced by Islamic art.

The top half of this cabinet opens by pulling down the entire upper panel to reveal ten drawers and two small inner doors, all with certosina decoration (see fig. 33–1). The top horizontal panel above the four drawers conceals two secret compartments. This cabinet, with its outer panel pulled down, could be used as a writing desk. *TJG*

1   William M. Odom, *History of Italian Furniture from the Fourteenth to the Early Nineteenth Centuries* (Garden City, N.Y.: Doubleday, Page, 1918–19; New York: Archive Press, reprint edition, 1966), fig. 71 on p. 82.
2   Illustrated in Odom, ibid., fig. 71 on p. 82, where it is listed as being in the collection of the Davanzati Palace, Florence.
3   French & Company stock sheet no. 53261-X (GRI Research Library, Los Angeles). A typewritten note from French & Company (in FIA curatorial file 2005.145) states that this cabinet was originally in the Davanzati Palace in Florence.
4   The certosina cabinet published as fig. 457 in Joseph Aronson, *The Encyclopedia of Furniture* (New York: Crown, reprint edition, 1962), n.p., is similar but not identical to the FIA's certosina cabinet, and also has a French & Company provenance; its present location is unknown. There is another certosina cabinet similar to the FIA's in the Virginia Museum of Fine Arts (67.54.4), which also has a French & Company provenance.

Fig. 33–1. Detail showing cat. 33 open

Sgabelli (cats. 34–36)

Sgabello (plural, *sgabelli*) means "stool" in Italian but came to be used for other types of chairs, including ones with backs.[1] The FIA's pair of sixteenth-century stools (cat. 34), with their plain rectangular tops and elaborately carved front and back supports, would have been objects to display with pride. Inspired by the ancient Greek and Roman art that was prized during the Renaissance, the grotesque masks, scrollwork with acanthus leaves, and lion's-paw feet create a lively yet carefully balanced ornamental base. This kind of stool, often used with a cushion, has been frequently depicted with important individuals seated upon them in paintings and engravings of this period.[2]

The front supports and seat backs of the set of sixteenth-century Italian *sgabelli* chairs (cat. 35) are also carved with elaborate design motifs. On the chairs' backs, S-shaped scrolls with vines flank a grotesque mask, surmounted by a Florentine lily. The scroll shapes are repeated on the bottom, where they flank cartouches bearing a painted coat of arms. With such detailed carving—the wood is pierced to give a sculptural effect—these chairs would have displayed the wealth and status of the family who owned them. This type of chair was also easy to move to different parts of the room. Because a room during this period had several functions, it was necessary to have furniture that could be moved to meet the needs of the occasion.[3] As with many pieces of Renaissance furniture and household objects, these chairs were more than just functional or even beautiful items:[4] the centrally placed coat of arms set within an elaborately carved cartouche conveyed the message that the family was both important and culturally refined, thus promoting its status.

The carved figures on the shaped backs of the sixteenth-century French *sgabelli* chairs (cat. 36) may have been based on drawings of acrobats by Italian and French artists working in the court of Francis I (r. 1515–47) at Fontainebleau.[5] Six semi-clad figures twist and turn in the confined space above two dolphin heads (fig. 36–1). Each back, though in the same format, is unique, with the figures in slightly different poses. The seats are also shaped and have a fluted rim. Each seat rests on two carved supports, composed of S-shaped scrolls flanking a cartouche containing a blank convex oval, with lion's-paw feet. *TJG*

Opposite: Fig. 36–1. Detail of cat. 36b, back of one of the French *sgabelli* chairs

1 Peter Thornton, *The Italian Renaissance Interior, 1400–1600* (London: Weidenfeld and Nicolson, 1991), pp. 168–69.

2 Ibid.

3 Elizabeth Currie, *Inside the Renaissance House* (London: Victoria and Albert Museum, 2006), pp. 24–25. Companion pieces to this pair are in the Cleveland Museum of Art, the Nelson-Atkins Museum of Art, Kansas City (33-18/1–2), and the Schloss Museum, Berlin; see Frida Schottmuller, *Furniture and Interior Decoration of the Italian Renaissance* (New York: Brentano's, 1921), p. 172 ill.

4 Currie, *Inside the Renaissance House*, pp. 13–14.

5 See George Szabo, *The Robert Lehman Collection* (New York: Metropolitan Museum of Art, 1975), p. 77, regarding the companion pieces in the Lehman Collection. He suggests the influence of the engravings of Giusto Betti or Juste de Juste. See also George Szabo, *Masterpieces of Italian Drawing in the Robert Lehman Collection* (New York: Hudson Hills Press, 1983), p. 58.

34.

Pair of *Sgabelli* Stools

Italian (Florence)

16th century

Wood, partly gilded

Each, 23 x 13 x 13³/₁₆ in.
(58.4 x 33 x 33.5 cm)

Gift of Viola E. Bray, 2005.131.1–2

Provenance: Stefano Bardini (1836–1922), Florence; purchased August 4, 1914 by French & Company, New York; sold to Mrs. A. B. Spreckles in 1914; returned to French & Company in 1930;[1] purchased May 30, 1958 by Viola E. Bray (1873–1961), Flint; gifted to Flint Board of Education in 1961 (housed at the FIA), transferred ownership to FIA in 2005.

Bibliography: Detroit 1958, no. 69, p. 37; Flint 1963.

1   French & Company stock sheet no. 5589 (GRI Research Library, Los Angeles).

Cat. 34a (opposite) and cat. 34b (right)

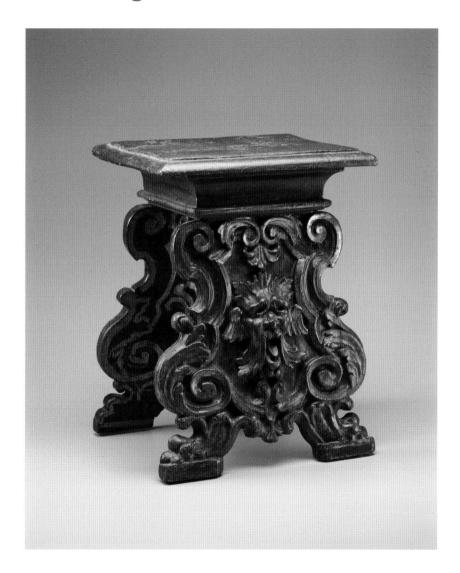

Pair of *Sgabelli* Chairs

Italian (Florence)

16th century

Walnut, partly gilded

Each, 39 x 13 x 17 in.
(33.5 x 33 x 43.2 cm)

Gift of Viola E. Bray, 2005.132.1–2

Provenance: Gerald Henry Foley, 7th Baron Foley (1898–1927), Ruxley Lodge, Claygate, Surrey, England; his sale in 1919, no. 235; Preston Pope Satterwhite (1867–1948); purchased April 6, 1939 by French & Company, New York;[1] purchased May 30, 1958 by Viola E. Bray (1873–1961), Flint; gifted to Flint Board of Education in 1961 (housed at the FIA), transferred ownership to FIA in 2005.

Bibliography: Flint 1963.

1 French and Company stock sheet, no. 41269 (GRI Research Library, Los Angeles) gives the following references: Ruxley Lodge Claygate Surrey catalogue, Oct. 1919, p. 16, no. 235; and *Art News* 31, no. 14 (December 31, 1932): 11.

Cat. 35a (opposite) and cat. 35b (right)

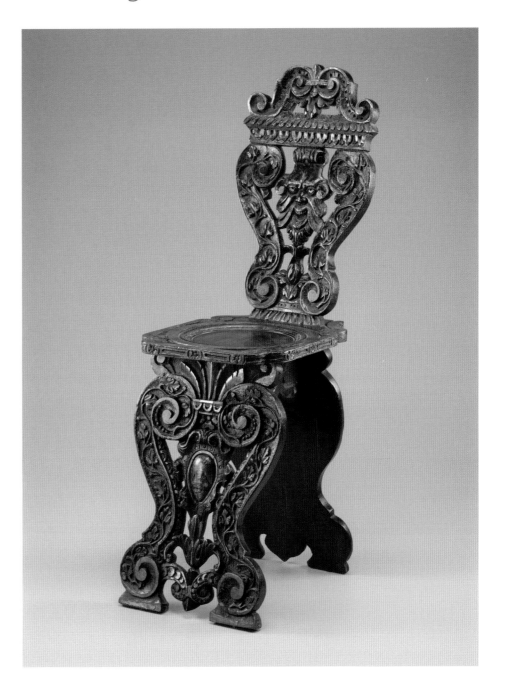

Pair of *Sgabelli* Chairs

Probably French
(Fontainebleau)

ca. 1550

Walnut

Each, 40 x 14 x 13$\frac{1}{2}$ in.
(101.6 x 35.6 x 34.3 cm)

Gift of Viola E. Bray, 2005.134.1–2

Provenance: Possibly Davanzati Palace, Florence;[1] Parke–Bernet Galleries, Hann sale, no. 639; purchased February 24, 1945 by French & Company, New York; purchased May 30, 1958 by Viola E. Bray (1873–1961), Flint; gifted to Flint Board of Education in 1961 (housed at the FIA), transferred ownership to FIA in 2005.

Bibliography: Detroit 1958, no. 75, p. 3; Flint 1963; Flint 1979, p. 12.

1   French & Company stock sheet no. 43222. (GRI Research Library, Los Angeles). A note from French & Company (in FIA curatorial file 2005.134.1–2) indicates that these stools were from the Davanzati Palace in Florence.

Cat. 36a (opposite) and cat. 36b (right)

Armchairs (cats. 37–39)
Pair of Carved Armchairs

Italian (Liguria)

16th century

Walnut with leather
and brass-headed nails

Each, 45 x 23 x 16 in.
(114.3 x 58.4 x 40.6 cm)

Gift of Viola E. Bray, 2005.133.1–2

Provenance: A. Seligman, Rey &
Co., New York; purchased March
15, 1930 by French & Company,
New York;[4] purchased May 30,
1958 by Viola E. Bray (1873–1961),
Flint; gifted to Flint Board of
Education in 1961 (housed at the
FIA), transferred ownership to FIA
in 2005.

Bibliography: Aronson 1962, ill.
fig. 213, listed as from French &
Company; Flint 1963.

Cat. 37a (opposite) and
cat. 37b (right)

A chair in an Italian Renaissance home was more than just a place to sit: it displayed the family's wealth, status, and cultural refinement. Chairs were often symbolic, with the largest and grandest being reserved for the most important person in the household, usually the father or an honored guest.[1] Materials, as well as carved ornament, were important in the construction of such an object. There were different types of chair designs available during the Renaissance period, as the works in the Bray collection attest.[2] These armchairs, with high rectangular backs, arms, and rear and side stretchers (cats. 37–39), became the basic prototype for the type of chair we still use today, unlike the *sgabelli* and Dantesca x-framed[3] chairs, which went out of fashion after the sixteenth century.

Chairs were often arranged against the walls of the reception rooms of the Renaissance interior, along with other large pieces of furniture. The arrangement of designs and ornaments on chairs usually reflected this placement. The front of chairs often received the most decoration, while the sides and back were usually left plain. *TJG*

1 Peter Thornton, *The Italian Renaissance
   Interior, 1400–1600* (London:
   Weidenfeld and Nicolson, 1991), p. 174.
2 The Bray collection contains two French
   chairs (not pictured) dated to the period
   of Henri II: armchair 2005.135 and
   caquetoire 2005.130.
3 The Bray collection contains two
   Dantesca chairs (not pictured): nos.
   2005.129 and 2005.139.
4 French & Company stock sheet no.
   36122 (GRI Research Library, Los
   Angeles).

Pair of Carved Armchairs

Italian (Tuscany)

16th or 17th century

Walnut with blue velvet
and gold-tasseled fringe

Each, 49 x 23 x 17 in.
(124.4 x 58.4 x 43.18 cm)

Gift of Viola E. Bray, 2005.137.1–2

Provenance: Possibly San
Domenico di Fiesole;[1] Mrs. I. D.
Levy; purchased January 11, 1937
by French & Company, New York;
purchased May 30, 1958 by Viola
E. Bray (1873–1961), Flint; gifted
to Flint Board of Education in 1961
(housed at the FIA), transferred
ownership to FIA in 2005.

1   French and Company stock sheet no.
    40564/8 (GRI Research Library, Los
    Angeles). A typewritten note from
    French & Company (in FIA curatorial
    file 2005.137.1–2) indicates that these
    two armchairs were from the "Villa San
    Dominic, Fiesole."

Cat. 38a (opposite) and
cat. 38b (right)

Pair of Carved Armchairs

Northern Italian

16th or 17th century

Walnut with blue velvet, gold silk appliqué, and gold-tasseled fringe

Each, 42 x 22½ x 17 in. (106.7 x 57.2 x 44.5 cm)

Gift of Viola E. Bray, 2005.138.1–2

Provenance: Luigi Orselli; purchased October 26, 1929 by French & Company, New York;[1] purchased May 30, 1958 by Viola E. Bray (1873–1961), Flint; gifted to Flint Board of Education in 1961 (housed at the FIA), transferred ownership to FIA in 2005.

1   French & Company stock sheet 35064 (GRI Research Library, Los Angeles).

Cat. 39a (opposite) and cat. 39b (right)

Prelate's Chair, or Hall Chair

French

16th century, period of Francis I
(r. 1515–47)

Walnut

74¹/₂ x 28 x 17³/₁₆ in.
(189.2 x 71.1 x 43.7 cm)

Gift of Viola E. Bray, 2005.136

Provenance: Possibly Émile Gavet
(1830–1904), Paris; Judge Elbert
Gary (1846–1927), New York;
French & Company, New York;[2]
purchased May 30, 1958 Viola E.
Bray (1873–1961), Flint; gifted to
Flint Board of Education in 1961
(housed at the FIA), transferred
ownership to FIA in 2005.

Bibliography: Flint 1963

A prelate's chair was often used for someone of high rank in the church, such as a bishop, but the same style of chair was also used by laypeople. Probably made under the reign of Francis I (r. 1515–47) in France, this chair has the old-fashioned Gothic boxlike form but embraces the new Renaissance style, with its carved ornament of rinceaux, flattened columns with stylized Corinthian capitals, and arms terminating in scrolls. The hinged seat could also be used for storage. This chair is also known as a throne stall.[1] *TJG*

1 Louise Ade Boger, *The Complete Guide to Furniture Styles* (New York: Scribner, 1969), p. 87.
2 Typewritten note from French & Company (in FIA curatorial file 2005.136).

Bibliography

Unpublished Documents

Note: *The unpublished documents cited in this book are from the library and curatorial files of the Flint Institute of Arts and from the archives of French & Company records in the Getty Research Institute Research Library, Los Angeles. For citations of these sources, the Flint Institute of Arts is abbreviated as* FIA, *and the Getty Research Institute is abbreviated as* GRI *and* GCPA. *Some of the unpublished FIA sources are referred to in full at first mention, and then abbreviated as follows:*

"FIA 1928–63"
"The Flint Institute of Arts: 1928 to 1963," anonymous undated typescript in FIA library.

"FIA First Five Years"
"The History of the First Five Years of the Founders Society of the Flint Institute of Arts," anonymous undated typescript in FIA library.

FIA, "The Bray Collection"
"The Bray Collection," anonymous undated typescript (1958 or later), FIA curatorial file 2005.124.

Published Texts

Ajmar-Wollheim, Marta, and Flora Dennis, eds. *At Home in Renaissance Italy*. London: Victoria and Albert Museum, 2006.

Alciati, Andrea. *A Book of Emblems: The Emblematum Liber in Latin and English*. Trans., ed., and with Introduction by John F. Moffitt. Jefferson, N.C.: McFarland, 2004.

Aronson, Joseph. *The Encyclopedia of Furniture*. New York: Crown, 1938; Crown, reprint edition, 1962.

Baudouin, Frans. *Rubens et son siècle*. Antwerp, Belgium: Mercator, 1972.

Baudoin, J[ean] (translator). *Iconologie, ou Explication Nouvelle de Plusieurs Images, Emblems, et autres Figures … Tirée des Recherches & des Figures de Cesar Ripa*. Paris: Mathieu Guillemot, 1644. Dijon: Faton, reprint edition, 1999.

Beckwith, A. *Majolica and Fayence: Italian, Sicilian, Majorcan, Hispano-Moresque and Persian*. New York: D. Appleton, 1877.

Belkin, Kristin Lohse. *Rubens*. London: Phaidon, 1998.

Bertrand, Pascal-François. *Les tapisseries des Barberini et la decoration d'intérieur dans la Rome baroque*. Turnhout, Belgium: Brepols, 2005.

———. "Une esposition de tapisseries à Rome pour le centenaire des Jesuites." *Antologia di Belle Arti: Studi sul Settecento II* (Turin, Italy), nos. 59–62 (2000): 154–66.

Boger, Louise Ade. *The Complete Guide to Furniture Styles*. New York: Scribner, 1969.

Bonnard, Marc, Beatrice Paolozzi Strozzi, and Nicholas Penny, eds. *Desiderio da Settignano: Sculptor of Renaissance Florence*. Exh. cat. Washington, D.C.: National Gallery of Art, 2007.

Boucher, Bruce, ed. *Earth and Fire: Italian Terracotta Sculpture from Donatello to Canova*. New Haven: Yale University Press, 2001.

Bray, Viola E. *Bray-Swart and Allied Families*. New York: The American Historical Company, 1941.

Opposite: Detail of cat. 31

Brejon de Lavergnée, Barbara. *Dessins de Simon Vouet, 1590–1649.* Paris: Réunion des Musées Nationaux, 1987.

Bremer-David, Charissa. "Building American Collections of European Tapestries: The Role and Influence of French and Company." Unpublished lecture at the Minneapolis Institute of Arts, 9 May 2002. Pdf. file accessed at http://tapestrycenter.org/wp-content/uploads/2008/12/4th-annual-lecture-bremer-david-transcript1.pdf.

———. "French & Company and American Collections of Tapestries, 1907–1959." *Studies in the Decorative Arts* (Fall–Winter 2003–4): 38–68.

Burchard, Ludwig, and Roger-Adolf d'Hulst. *Rubens Drawings.* Vol. 1. Brussels: Arcade, 1963.

Caiger-Smith, Alan. *Tin-Glaze Pottery.* London: Faber and Faber, 1973.

Campbell, Thomas P. *Tapestry in the Renaissance: Art and Magnificence.* New York: Metropolitan Museum of Art, 2002.

Catalogue of the Renowned Collection of Works of Art, Chiefly Formed by the Late Hollingworth Magniac, Esq. (Known as the Colworth Collection). July 2 and July 4, 1892.

Christian, Kathleen Wren. "Instauratio and Pietas: The della Valle Collections of Ancient Sculpture." In Nicholas Penny and Eike D. Schmidt, eds., *Collecting Sculpture in Early Modern Europe.* Washington, D.C.: National Gallery of Art, 2008.

"Coming Auctions, Twombly Sale, Part 2." *Art News*, 54, no. 1 (Summer [June, July, August] 1955): 66.

Coural, Jean. *Chefs-d'œuvre de la Tapisserie Parisienne 1597–1662.* Exh. cat. Versailles: Orangerie de Versailles, 1967.

Crelly, William R. *The Painting of Simon Vouet.* New Haven and London: Yale University Press, 1962.

Currie, Elizabeth. *Inside the Renaissance House.* London: Victoria and Albert Museum. 2006.

Dacos, Nicole. *The Loggia of Raphael: A Vatican Art Treasure.* Trans. Josephine Bacon. New York: Abbeville Press, 2008.

Darr, Alan Phipps, Peter Barnet, Antonia Boström, et al. *Catalogue of Italian Sculpture in the Detroit Institute of Arts.* Detroit: Detroit Institute of Arts, 2002.

Delmarcel, Guy. *Flemish Tapestry.* New York: Harry N. Abrams, 1999.

Delmarcel, Guy, Nicole de Reyniès, and Wendy Hefford. *The Toms Collection: Tapestries of the Sixteenth to Nineteenth Centuries*, ed. Giselle Eberhard Cotton. Trans. Irena Podleska and Geoffrey Peek. Lausanne, Switz.: Fondation Toms Pauli, and Zurich and Sulgen, Switz.: Niggli, 2010.

Demonts, Louis. "Les Amours de Renaud et d'Armide, décoration peinte par Simon Vouet pour Claude de Bullion." *Bulletin de la Société de l'Histoire de l'Art Francais* (Paris, 1913): 58–78.

Denis, Isabelle. "The Parisian Workshops, 1590–1650" and entry no. 13: "Diana and Apollo Slaying the Children of Niobe." In *Tapestry in the Baroque: Threads of Splendor*, ed. Thomas P. Campbell. Exh. cat. New York: Metropolitan Museum of Art, 2007.

―――. "Tenture de l'Ancien Testament," "Les Travaux d'Ulysse," and "Les Amours des Dieux." In *Lisses et délices: Chefs-d'oeuvre de la tapisserie de Henri IV à Louis XIV*. Exh. cat. Paris: Caisse Nationale des monuments historiques et des sites, 1996.

Detroit 1958
Decorative Arts of the Italian Renaissance 1400–1600. Exh. cat., Detroit: Detroit Institute of Arts, 1958.

Evers, Hans Gerhard. *Peter Paul Rubens*. Munich: F. Bruckmann, 1942.

Fenaille, Maurice et al. *État-général des tapisseries de la Manufacture des Gobelins depuis son origine jusqu'à nos jours, 1600–1900. Les Ateliers Parisiens au Dix-Septième Siècle depuis l'installation de Marc de Comans et de François de La Planche au Faubourg Saint-Marcel in 1601 jusqu'à la Fondation de la Manufacture royale des meubles de la Couronne en 1662*. Vol. 1. Paris: Imprimerie nationale, 1923.

Ferguson, George. *Signs and Symbols in Christian Art: With Illustrations from Paintings of the Renaissance*. Oxford: Oxford University Press, 1976.

Ffoulke, Charles M. *The Barberini Tapestries: Armida and Rinaldo Series at "Florham," Convent, New Jersey*. Ed. and rev. by Cushing Stetson. New York: privately printed by J. J. Little and Ives, 1930.

―――. *The Ffoulke Collection of Tapestries*. New York: privately printed, 1913.

Flint 1963
The Viola E. Bray Renaissance Gallery. Flint: Flint Institute of Arts, 1963.

Flint 1979
Flint Institute of Arts: Highlights from the Collections. Flint: Flint Institute of Arts, 1979.

Freemantle, Katharine. *The Baroque Town Hall of Amsterdam*. Utrecht: Haentjens Dekker & Gumbert, 1959.

Geck, Francis J. *French Interiors and Furniture: The Period of Francis I*. Roseville, Mich.: Stureck Educational Services, 1982.

Gerard, John. *The Herbal or General History of Plants, The Complete 1633 Edition as Revised and Enlarged by Thomas Johnson*. London, 1633. New York: Dover Publications, reprint edition, 1975.

Gere, J. A. "Taddeo Zuccaro as a Designer for Maiolica," *Burlington Magazine* 105, no. 724 (July 1963): 306–15.

Gombrich, E. H. *Symbolic Images: Studies in the Art of the Renaissance*. 2nd ed. London: Phaidon, 1978.

Grimal, Pierre. *The Dictionary of Classical Mythology*. Trans. A. R. Maxwell-Hyslop. Oxford and New York: Blackwell, 1986.

Gruber, Alain. *The History of Decorative Arts: The Renaissance and Mannerism in Europe*. New York: Abbeville Press, 1994.

Guiffrey, Jules. *Inventaire général du Mobilier de la Couronne sous Louis XIV (1663–1715)*. Paris: Société d'Encouragement pour la propagation des livre d'art, 1885.

Hall, James. *Dictionary of Subjects and Symbols in Art*. London: J. Murray, 1974; New York: Harper & Row, paperback edition, 1979.

Haskell, Francis and Nicholas Penny. *Taste and the Antique: The Lure of Classical Sculpture, 1500–*

1900. New Haven and London: Yale University Press, 1981.

Herluison, Henri. *Actes d'etat-civil d'artistes français peintres, graveurs, architectes, etc.* Orléans, 1873; Geneva: Slatkine, reprint edition, 1972.

Hoff, Ursula. "A Tapestry from a Painting by Simon Vouet." *Art Bulletin of Victoria* (1971–72): 25–29.

Hunter, George Leland. *The Practical Book of Tapestries.* Philadelphia and London: J. B. Lippincott, 1925.

Jestaz, Bertrand. "La Tapisserie française, 1597–1662." *Revue de l'Art*, no. 1/2. Paris: Flammarion, 1968.

Kelly, Raymond J., III. *To Be, Or Not To Be: Four Hundred Years of Vanitas Painting.* Flint: Flint Institute of Arts, 2006.

Koeppe, Wolfram. "French and Italian Renaissance Furniture at the Metropolitan Museum of Art," *Apollo* 138 (1994): 30.

Lami, Stanislas. *Dictionnaire des sculpteurs de l'école française sous le règne de Louis XIV.* Paris: H. Champion, 1906.

Larsen, Erik. *P. P. Rubens with a Complete Catalogue of His Works in America.* Antwerp: De Sikkel, 1952.

Lavalle, Denis. "Simon Vouet et le tapisserie," and "La Tenture de Renaud et Armide." In *Vouet*, ed. Jacques Thuillier. Exh. cat. Paris: Galeries nationales du Grand Palais, 1990.

Lawrence, Cynthia. "Before *The Raising of the Cross*: The Origins of Rubens's Earliest Antwerp Altarpieces." *Art Bulletin* 81, no. 2 (June 1999): 267–96.

———. "Rubens's *Raising of the Cross* in Context: the 'Early Christian' Past and the Evocation of the Sacred in Post-Tridentine Antwerp." Chapter 12 in *Defining the Holy: Sacred Space in Medieval and Early Modern Europe.* Ed. by Andrew Spicer and Sarah Hamilton. Aldershot, U.K.: Ashgate, 2005.

Lee, Rensselaer W. *Ut Pictura Poesis: The Humanistic Theory of Painting.* New York: W. W. Norton, 1967.

Lisses et délices: Chefs-d'oeuvre de la tapisserie de Henri IV á Louis XIV. Paris: Caisse Nationale des monuments historiques et des sites, 1996.

Malvern, Marjorie M. *Venus in Sackcloth: The Magdalen's Origins and Metamorphoses.* Carbondale: Southern Illinois University Press, 1975.

Marquand, Allan. *Giovanni della Robbia.* Princeton: Princeton University Press, 1920.

Martin, John Rupert. "The Angel from Rubens's 'Raising of the Cross.'" In *Rubens and His World.* Ed. by Roger Adolf d'Hulst. Antwerp: Het Gulden Cabinet, 1985.

———. *Rubens: The Antwerp Altarpieces.* New York: W. W. Norton, 1969.

Moseley, Charles. *A Century of Emblems: An Introductory Anthology.* Aldershot, Eng.: Scolar Press, 1989.

Motture, Peta, ed. *Large Bronzes in the Renaissance.* New Haven, Conn.: Yale University Press, 2003.

Odom, William M. *History of Italian Furniture from the Fourteenth to the Early Nineteenth Century.* 2 vols. 1918. Garden City, N.Y.: Doubleday, Page, 1918–19; New York: Archive Press, reprint edition, 1966.

Panofsky, Erwin. *Studies in Iconology: Humanistic Themes in the Art of the Renaissance*. New York: Harper & Row, [1962], 1972 paperback edition (reprint of original 1939 Oxford University Press edition).

Paoletti, John T., and Gary M. Radke. *Art in Renaissance Italy*. New York: Abrams, 1997; Upper Saddle River, N.J.: Prentice Hall, paperback edition, 1997.

Petrucci, Francesca, Giancarlo Gentilini, and Fiamma Domestici. *Della Robbia*. Milan: Giunti, 1999.

Poke, Christopher. "Jacques Androuet I Ducerceau's 'Petites Grotesques' as a Source for Urbino Maiolica Decoration." *Burlington Magazine* 143, no. 1179 (June 2001): 332–44.

Ripa, Cesare. *Baroque and Rococo Pictorial Imagery: The 1758–60 Hertel Edition of Ripa's* Iconologia *with 200 Engraved Illustrations*. Ed. and with Introduction by Edward A. Maser. New York: Dover, 1971.

Rolland, Victor, Johannes Baptista Rietstap, and Henri Rolland. *V. & H. V. Rolland's Illustrations to the Armorial General*. 6 vols. in 3. Baltimore: Heraldic Book Co., and London: Heraldry Today, reprint edition, 1967.

Rooses, Max. *L'Oeuvre de P. P. Rubens: Histoire et description de ses tableaux et dessins*. Vol. 2. Antwerp: J. Maes, 1888.

Rossi, Paola. *Girolamo Campagna*. Verona: Vita Veronese, 1968.

Schottmuller, Frida. *Furniture and Interior Decoration of the Italian Renaissance*. New York: Brentano's, 1921.

Schulz, Anne Markham. "One Old, and Nine New, Attributions to Giovanni Buora." *Rivista d'Arte* (new series) no. 1 (2011): 39–77.

Sheard, Wendy Stedman. *Antiquity in the Renaissance*, vol. 2, n.p. Exh. cat. Northampton, Mass.: Smith College Museum of Art, 1978.

Standen, Edith. "Tapisseries Renaissance, maniéristes et baroques: nouveaux developments." *Revue de l'Art* 22 (1973): 91–97.

Szabo, George. *Masterpieces of Italian Drawing in the Robert Lehman Collection*. New York: Hudson Hills Press, 1983.

———. *The Robert Lehman Collection*. New York: Metropolitan Museum of Art, 1975.

Tasso, Torquato. *Gerusalemme Liberata*. Parma, Italy, 1581. Trans. by Edward Fairfax as *Jerusalem Delivered*, first published in London: A. Hatfield for J. Jaggard and M. Lownes, 1600. Project Gutenberg Etext, January 1995: www.gutenberg.org/dirs/3/9/392/392.txt, posted August 4, 2008.

———. *Jerusalem Delivered (Gerusalemme Liberata)*. Ed. and trans. by Anthony M. Esolen. Baltimore: Johns Hopkins University Press, 2000.

Thornton, Peter. *The Italian Renaissance Interior, 1400–1600*. London: Weidenfeld and Nicolson, 1991.

Thuillier, Jacques. "Introduction." In *Chefs-d'oeuvre de la Tapisserie Parisienne, 1597–1662*. Ed. Jean Coural. Exh. cat. Versailles: Orangerie de Versailles, 1967.

Thuillier, Jacques, Barbara Brejon de Lavergnée, and Denis Lavalle. *Vouet*. Exh. cat. Paris: Galeries Nationales du Grand Palais, 1990.

Tinagli, Paola. *Women in Italian Renaissance Art: Gender, Representation, Identity.* Manchester: Manchester University Press, 1997.

Unglaub, Jonathan. *Poussin and the Poetics of Painting: Pictorial Narrative and the Legacy of Tasso.* Cambridge and New York: Cambridge University Press, 2006.

Vasari, Giorgio. *Lives of the Painters, Sculptors, and Architects.* Trans. Julia Conaway Bondanella and Peter Bondanella. Oxford: Oxford University Press, 1998.

Vignon, Charlotte. *Exuberant Grotesques: Renaissance Maiolica from the Fontana Workshop.* New York: Frick Collection, 2009.

Vittet, Jean. Entry no. 15: "Moses Rescued from the Nile." In *Tapestry in the Baroque: Threads of Splendor*, ed. Thomas P. Campbell, pp. 163–69. Exh. cat. New York: Metropolitan Museum of Art, in association with Yale University Press, 2007.

Vittet, Jean, and Arnauld Brejon de Lavergnée, with Monique de Savignac. *La collection de tapisseries de Louis XIV.* Dijon: Faton, 2010.

Weiss, Roberto. *The Renaissance Discovery of Classical Antiquity.* 2nd ed. Oxford: Basil Blackwell, 1988.

Wilson, Timothy. *Italian Maiolica of the Renaissance.* Milan: Bocca, 1996.

Wind, Edgar. *Pagan Mysteries in the Renaissance.* New York: Norton, 1968.

Zaho, Margaret Ann. *Imago Triumphalis: The Function and Significance of Triumphal Imagery for Italian Renaissance Rulers.* New York: Peter Lang, 2004.

Index

This index includes:
- Names of artists, patrons, collectors, galleries, and museums represented in the collection;
- Objects by title, type, featured subject, and motif;
- Allegorical and moral themes represented in the imagery; and
- Allegorical and mythological figures and muses represented in the objects, along with
- Their symbols and attributes

Latona, Roman goddess, mother of Diana and Apollo, 109

laurel wreath, 87; symbol of victory and virtuous love, 36; refers to Apollo, 36

Laurent, Girard, master tapestry weaver, 37

Laurent, Girard, the Younger, 34, 39

Lavalle, Denis, Vouet exhibition curator, 46

Le Brun, Jean-Baptiste-Pierre, French painter, printmaker, 87

Learning (allegorical figure), 24

Leonardo da Vinci, Italian artist, 15

Lerambert, Henri, French painter, *Artemisia* or *Coriolanus*, 48

Leszczyńska, Marie, queen consort of Louis XV, 13

Levis, Giuseppe de, Veronese sculptor-bronze founder, pair of altar candlesticks (cat. 18) attrib. to, 107

Levy, Mrs. I. D., 157

lightning bolt, on two-part cabinet (cat. 32), 142

lily, symbol of purity: Florentine, on *sgabelli* chairs (cat. 35), 147, *150–51*

Linlithgow, Marquis of, 91

lion, attributes of: power and strength, 22; watchfulness and guardianship, 23; detail of cat. 31 (fig. 16), *23*

lion's heads or masks: on wine cistern (cat. 12), 23, *91*, 92; on andirons (cat. 22), *116*, 117; on *cassoni* (cat. 24), 124; on *credenza* (cat. 26), *130*; carved on cabinet drawers of two-part cabinet (cat. 31) *141*, 142

lion's-head and -paw supports, on wine cistern (cat. 12), 23, *91*, 92

lion's-mask pulls, on *credenza* (cat. 26), *130*

lion's-paw feet: on *cassoni* (cat. 24), 22, 23, *120*, 121; on *credenza* (cat. 26), *130*; on octagonal table (cat. 28), *134*, 135; on library table (cat. 30), *138*, 139; on *sgabelli* (cats. 34, 36), 147, *148*, *149*, *152*, *153*

Lombardo, Pietro, Venetian sculptor, architect: pair of candlesticks (cat. 15) attrib. to, 4; 101

Lombardo family, architectural projects by, 101

looms and weavers, workshop arrangement of, 40

Louis XIII, king of France, 7, 32, 33, 45, 47

Louis XIV, king of France, 47, 50

love, theme represented in context of Bray collection, 20: celestial and earthly, 25, 36; represented by Venus, 22, 25; sacred and profane, 127; love and lust, 25; lyric love and poetry, virtuous love and compassion, 35, 36

Loves of the Gods, The, by Vouet, 45

Lucy, Countess of Egmont, 13

Luna, moon goddess, identified with Diana, 109

lust, symbolized in art, 20, 25

lyre, attribute of Apollo, patron of poetry and music, *110*, *111*

Mackay, Clarence H., 4, 10, 101, 121, 135, 141

Magdalene, Figure of the, olive wood, by Nanques (cat. 20), 4, 26, *112*, 113

Magniac, Hollingworth, Esq., 127

maiolica (also: majolica): 7, tin-glazed earthenware, 99; pair of vases (cat. 13), *94*, 95; wine cistern (cat. 12), 10, 22, *90*, *91*, 92; (fig. 9), *12*; Deruta vase (cat. 14), *98*, 99

Majorca, Island of (formerly Isola di Majolica), 95

maniera all'antica (decoration in the ancient manner, style of antiquity), 21; acanthus leaves, garlands, organic motifs, palmettes, rinceaux, and wreaths, 22

Mannerism, Mannerist, 92, 143

mantelpiece, armorial, 16th-century French (cat. 23), *118*, 119;

Mars, Roman god of war, 22, (fig. 14), *23*, 39; in allegories of Peace, 22; in tapestries and cartouches (cats. 1, 6, 7, 9), 22, 37; *54*, *55*, *70*, *71*, *72*, *73*, *78*, 79

Martelli Palace, Florence, 131, 139

Martelli, Roberto, early patron of Donatello, 139

mask(s): angel with wings, on *cassoni* bases (cat. 24), *120*; cherub, on two-part cabinet (cat.

31), *9*, 141; on ceramic vases (cat. 13), *94*, 95; female, on *cassoni* (cat. 24), *120*; female, carved on two-part cabinet (cat. 31, fig. 31–2), *141*, *162*; grotesque, on andirons (cat. 22), 117, 118; on *sgabelli* (cats. 34 and 35), *146*, 147, *148*, 149

Mazarin, Jules, cardinal, 84

McKown Twombly, Mrs. Hamilton (born Florence Vanderbilt), 4, 10, 84

Medici family, Florentine art patrons, 92

Medici, Marie de', mother and regent of Louis XIII, 47

Medusa, head or face of, on Minerva's shield, *24*, 39, *140*, 141; on tapestry cartouches (cats. 2, 5), 57, 58, *66*, 67; on two-part cabinet (cat. 31), *140*, 141

memento mori. See skull

Mercury (Greek Hermes): *24*; as patron of travelers, 39; as Roman messenger-god, 24; in tapestry cartouches (cats. 2, 5), 24, 56, 57, 66, 67; winged feet and helmet, *24*; winged feet and caduceus, 39; and wisdom, 24

Metropolitan Museum of Art, New York, 4, 5, 37, 135

Michelangelo, influence on Rubens, 89

Middle Ages, 99

Minerva (Greek Athena), Roman goddess of wisdom and warfare: *24*, 39, 141; attributes of: helmet, shield, spear, 24; goddess of war and wisdom, 24; patroness of arts, learning, crafts, 24; on two-part cabinet door (cat. 31), *140*, 141; with owl, 23; with spear and shield with Medusa, 39, *140*, 141; in tapestry cartouches (cats. 2, 5), *24*, 56, 57, 58, *66*, 67; Judgment of Paris (cat. 13a), *6*, 97

mirror, attribute of Prudence, 26, (fig. 17) 37; Armida's, *66*, 67; details, (fig. 5–1), *67*, (fig. 6–1), *71*; on parcel-gilded cabinet with young male (cat. 25b, fig. 25–3), *128*

Mobilier National (formerly Garde-Meuble de la Couronne), 4, 40, 42

Tasso, Torquato, Tuscan poet. See *Gerusalemme Liberata (Jerusalem Delivered)*

Tayer, Jean (also known as Hans Taye), tapestry weaver, 40

telamon, male figure as sculptural support: 21; (fig. 6), *34*; in drawing by van Heemskerck, *Courtyard in the old Palazzo*, (fig. 7), *34*; on vase (cat. 13b, fig. 13–1), *96*

Temperance (allegorical figure), cardinal virtue, 26, 36

Tempesta, Antonio, etching by, (fig. 5), *33*

term(s) (or herm[s] pillar figure[s]): 21, on *credenza* (cat. 26), *130, 131*; on two-part cabinet (cat. 31, detail, fig. 31–1), *140, 141*

Terpsichore (muse of dancing and song), 24

Thalia (muse of comedy), 24

themes represented in Bray collection: abundance and fruitfulness, 20, 28; agility and fleetness, 39; belief in the divine, 31; conversion and redemption, 81; courage and strength, 26; dancing and song, 24; duty versus desire, 31; earth and agriculture, 28; faith and virtue, 20, 26; fertility and fruitfulness, flora and fauna, force and valor, love and lust, 20; malevolence and dark magic, 31; power and fertility, 28; power and status, 20, 22; power and strength, 23; rest and repose, 31; sacred and profane, 127; seasons (change of), 124; secular and sacred, 7; unity and concord, 28; valor and action, 31; virtue and military concord, 39; watchfulness and guardianship, 23; wisdom and secret knowledge, 20, 23; worldly strife and death, 35. *See also* love, and virtues, cardinal

throne stall. *See* chair, prelate's (cat. 40)

Thuillier, Jacques, 1967 tapestry exhibition catalogue author, 45

tiara, papal (three-tiered crown), 129; depicted on parcel-gilded cabinets (cat. 25), *126, 127*; (figs. 25–1, 25–2), *127, 128*

tin-glazed earthenware, 91, 95, 99, 105. *See also* maiolica

Thou, Jacques-Auguste de, tapestry patron, collector, 47

Titian, Venetian painter, influence on Rubens, 89

Tobias, biblical figure, life of, depicted on *cassoni* (cat. 24), 120–23

Tobit apochryphal book of the Bible, 121; father of Tobias, 122

tragedy, muse of, Melpomene, 24

Trionfi (Triumphs), poem by Petrarch, 127

Trojan War, 97

trumpet, attribute of Calliope (muse of epic poetry), 24; attribute of Fame (allegorical figure), 24; winged figure blowing trumpet, 127, 129

trumpeting figure, depicted on parcel-gilded cabinets (cat. 25), *126, 127*

Two heads of a man capped with a helmet, sketch by Vouet, (fig. 2), *48*

Two studies of the head of Rinaldo tilted back towards the left, drawing by Vouet, (fig. 8), *35*

Twombly, Mrs. Hamilton McKown (born Florence Vanderbilt), 4, 10, 84

Twombly, Ruth Vanderbilt, daughter of Mrs. Hamilton McKown Twombly (Florence Vanderbilt), 84

Ubaldo, knight depicted in tapestries. *See* Carlo and Ubaldo

United Distillers of America, 137

Urania, muse of astronomy (fig. 1), *viii*, *1*; with armillary sphere, compass, a crown of stars, 24; (fig. 15), *37*; (fig. 19), *38*, 39; (cats. 4, 6, 8, 10), *62, 63, 70, 71, 76, 77, 80, 81*

Urban VIII, Pope, residences of his nephews, 47

Urbino, Italy, 10, 92, 95

valor in combat, 36

Van Boucle, Pierre, assistant painter to Vouet, 35

van Heemskerck, Maerten, Dutch painter, 34

van Westwezel, Heer, 87

Vanderbilt, Florence. *See* Twombly, Mrs. Hamilton McKown

Vandrisse, François, 48

vase, (Deruta maiolica), (cat. 14), *98*, 99

vases, pair of, style of Fontana family (cat. 13), 23, *94*, 95; (fig. 1), *6*, detail of backs (figs. 13–1, 13–2), *96, 97*

Venus, Roman goddess of love, 22, 25, 26, 95, 127; details (cat. 25a): 25, *126, 127, 128, 129*; as profane love, in chariot on parcel-gilded cabinet (cat. 25a, fig. 25–1), 25, *127*; swan attribute, on parcel-gilded on cabinet (cat. 25a, fig. 25–1), *127*; attributes in tapestry (cat. 5), 25, *66, 67*; Judgment of Paris (cat. 13a, fig.1 and fig. 13–2), *7*, 97

Victoria (Victory) (allegorical figure), 39; (fig. 16), 37; personification of worldly achievement, 39; (fig. 15), 37; symbolized by laurel wreath, 39; in tapestry cartouches (cats. 4, 7, and 10), *62, 63, 72, 73, 80, 81, 85*

Vinck, Baron de, 87

vine(s), leafy scrolling: on lids of *cassoni* (cat. 24), *120, 121*; on octagonal table leg (cat. 28), *134, 135*; on *sgabelli* (cat. 35), *150, 151*. *See also* rinceaux

Viola E. Bray Gallery, *vi–vii*; *1, 2, 7–11*. *See also* Bray, Viola Estella

Virgil, classical Roman poet, 31

virtues, cardinal; (Fortitude, Prudence, Justice, Temperance), in *The Story of Rinaldo and Armida* tapestries (except Temperance) 26, 36, 39. *See* Fortitude, Prudence, Justice

Visconti, Spain, coat of arms on mantelpiece (cat. 23), *118, 119*

Vittet, Jean, author, article on Vouet tapestry, *Moses Rescued from the Nile*, 47

Volpi, Elia, Florentine antiques dealer, 133

Vouet, Simon, French painter, *premier peintre*